Enrichment
of the
Self and Soul

RICHARD J. CHOURA

Book
Collaborators
Your Story, Our Network

ENRICHMENT OF THE SELF AND SOUL
Copyright © 2025 Richard J. Choura

ISBN 978-1-967362-59-2 (Paperback)
ISBN 978-1-967362-60-8 (Ebook)
ISBN 978-1-967362-61-5 (Hardcover)

Printed in the United States of America

CONTENTS

ABOUT THE BOOK

The world is turning metaphysical today, and it is the purpose of this book to show you how to part the metaphysical curtain and see the sense of the mysterious, the poetical, and the mystical in the first principles and structures of Nature, the Universe, and the self. Today, knowledge has been accumulated in countless written, graphic, and digital forms but there are still a number of metaphysical questions such as:

"If the Universe has a heartbeat, why does its heart rate depend on the hearer?"

"What deeper revelations in the sciences, art, philosophy, religion, literature, psychology, physiology, biology, or music allow me to enrich the meaning of my self, my soul, and my existence. What is the self? How is it important? What makes it special? What causes it to change? How can I add metaphysical dimensions to my everyday life?"

For many of us, the purpose of life is to overcome randomness, nothingness, or sameness, to establish a personal identity of self, and to find meaning in a meaningless world. We struggle to keep life from being merely a passage from some kind of physical order to some kind of novelty. We strive to keep life from becoming a coordinated inheritance of mental novelties. We seek to know the world lest we become its prey.

The purpose of this book is to answer the above metaphysical questions, achieve the above purposes, and help the reader relate constructively to the contrasting qualities of:

A. Body vs. self

B. Matter vs. spirit

C. Self-consciousness vs. Cosmic consciousness

Today, images of chaos and social disintegration are often in our thoughts and in the news. Life is like a "monumental space ruled by chaos." We are confronted often with financial crisis, unemployment, changing technology, war, and loss of family and friends. We live in a world that is condemned to perpetual change. It is as if misfortune and change were the work of the devil and lack of harmony and order were caused by sin. As a result, we struggle with the inward drama of the soul to establish a world which is meaningful and peaceful. In the midst of our "topsy-turvy world" we find that the human condition requires an occasional act of heroism to overcome our sorrow, loneliness, or despair.

Genetic engineering, cloning, and genomic science are redefining our evolution and existence and the relation of our self, soul, and spirit to the world around us, the universe, and God. Some of these events may cause us to feel isolated from God or from our soul and so we may need to ask "Does one's spirit lie deeper within the self- and if so- what does that mean if were to be cloned or genetically engineered? Would cloning or genetic engineering hide God from us? It has recently been discovered that for an implanted cell to develop, the genes that were turned off for cloning purposes must be turned on again in order to guide the egg to form a new, genetically identical individual. Scientist have found that genes can easily be incompletely reprogrammed and lead to problems. In view of these things, it seems urgent that we come to understand the self with immediacy and with clarity.

This book immediately reveals what the elements of self are, how the self relates to the mysteriousness of the universe, and ideas which enrich one's self and soul. It is said that in order to create a great work of art such as in music or in painting, one must understand the principles, and to touch the emotions one must know the elements. And so, this book provides the reader with the principles and elements of self so that the reader can create an enriched and satisfying self.

Henry Miller wrote:

"The new work of art does not consist of making a living or producing an object d'art or in self therapy, but in finding a new soul. The new era is the era of spiritual creativity …and soul making."

READER BENEFITS

Once you choose "Enrichment of the Self and Soul":

1. The reader will experience spiritual growth by learning how they themselves can be part of higher achievements connecting examples and patterns of the physical and spiritual world related to art, religion, psychology, science, philosophy, music, and literature.

2. The reader will feel more filled with spirituality and in touch with their intuitive powers so that they can change their life for the better as they key in on activities and aims that are closer to their essence.

3. The reader will experience more moments that change their life for the better.

4. The reader will be able to mold their life into a meaningful if not amazing journey.

5. The reader will learn new sources of spirituality and be able to connect their spirituality to their everyday lives.

6. The reader will acquire a wide variety of enthusiastic visions that extend their spirit and fill up the "gaps of human life with light." The reader will thus able to see "the secrets of the far."

7. The reader will be boosted spiritually, metaphysically, aesthetically, and psychologically to reach a new union with mind, self, and soul.

INTRODUCTION

T he concept of self helps us value the miracle of existence. It has the capacity to open existence to transcendence. This book deals with the concept of self versus the concepts of finite matter, time, space, entropy, spirituality, and infinity. These will be discussed so that the reader may become a metaphysical participant in the modern world. To become metaphysical is to become learned about the principles of one's existence, time,being, the structure of nature, the cosmos, and self. By comparing the self to the other concepts mentioned above, we can appreciate the depth, dynamics, and mysteriousness of existence. Albert Einstein stated:

"The most beautiful and deepest experience a man and woman can have is the sense of the mysterious. It is the underlying principle of religion as well as of all serious endeavor in art and science … He or she who never had this experience seems to me if not dead, then at least blind. The sense that behind anything that can be experienced there is something that our mind cannot grasp and whose beauty and sublimity reaches us only indirectly and as feeble reflection, this is religiousness. In this sense I am religious. To me it suffices to wonder at these secrets and to attempt humbly to grasp with my mind a mere image of the lofty structure of all there is."

To grasp the lofty structure of all there is, we search the vast mysteries which surround our little island of knowledge, and determine what is significant and what is not. We bring into harmony the forces of faith and reason with the help of science and philosophy. We use reason to discover in action what is good. Some have called reason "an organ for discovering truth" or a channel of discovery. We use faith to strengthen us as we venture into opposition, difficulty, or discouragement. Faith in order is the basis of science. Science has sometimes been said to be opposed to faith, and inconsistent with it. But, all science, in fact rests on a basis of faith, for it assumes the permanence and uniformity of natural laws-a thing, which cannot always be demonstrated.

In searching the vast mysteries, which surround us, we ask ourselves two questions: What is the world look like? What is the situation of my self in the world?

To answer these questions, we use philosophy and science. Science tells us what our world is like and philosophy helps us understand what our self is like in the world. The branch of philosophy, which discusses the science of being and the origin and the structure of the universe (cosmology), is metaphysics the branch we are most concerned with. French poet, Jean De Bouffler's wrote: "Metaphysics is the anatomy of the soul."

Metaphysics is about the way we think about the world. In metaphysics, we ask what criteria must a person have to be an individual or have a self - Are there some essential properties - What distinguishes one particular person from another. Man and woman cannot compare themselves with any other creature; they are not an ape, kangaroo, or a tree. If we are a splinter of some infinite deity, how can we best form a definite opinion of ourselves - Our abilities have such a range that we are almost like mythical beings. It is said that mythology is like religious sentiment gone wild. Mythology is not religion, of course, but we might ask ourselves if we are a poetical counterpart of dogmatic theology when we try to form a definite opinion of ourselves.

As a particular event, we know that life passes so fast it is surprising that anything develops at all. Life is filled with unending growth and decay. Yet, there is an enduring something that lives under the eternal flux of life. That enduring something is our inner experiences and self. Of course, there are outward circumstances, but they are seldom a substitute for inner experiences. Through inner experiences, man and woman are raised out of the animal world, and by their minds they demonstrate that nature has put a premium on the development of consciousness. Through consciousness, we take possession of nature by recognizing the existence of the world.

We would ask that metaphysics give us a picture of the self in the world in a way that satisfies our deep need to add meaning to our existence, our soul search, and our quest for spiritual growth. In recent times, science has undergone considerable revolutionary changes, which say that the world is different than we thought and that there are new intriguing answers to our philosophical questions. Some of these changes tell us that the universe is expanding, that matter and energy are not separate, and that Newton's Laws are no longer the guideline in science or philosophy that they once were.

It has been determined that the Newtonian law of mechanics is not consistent with the second law of thermodynamics. To solve this problem, a physicist named Oswald recommended the fundamental term mass be replaced with the term energy. Thus, the laws of physics became the law of entrophy rather than the law of mechanics. This lead Ostwald to proclaim:

"We have eliminated the last horrible gap between matter and spirit which remained from times of Descartes." This viewpoint also included the idea that whenever nature or humans act, that act is irreversible: and what is done is done forever. As a result, it was also concluded that the laws of physics should be based on energy rather than mechanics if the development of science was to progress."

Since the above occurrence, science has created novel methods for discovering facts, which have uncovered gaps in our previous knowledge and uncovered new knowledge. Philosophy has reconciled things with other things and minds with other minds. This book reconciles things with self and soul, minds with self and soul, and promotes enrichment of the dimensions, depth, direction, and dynamics of the self and soul.

We start with the questions: What should the stuff in my mind represent - What is there about Nature of the Cosmos that can enrich my Reason and Reality - What is closer to me than myself - Do I know more about others than myself - What kind of being do I want to make of myself. The purpose of this book is to furnish creative, poetical, and "realizing" answers.

In the new age, much of physics and reality is non-deterministic, involves considerations of probability, and is sometimes reduced tostatistical laws, as well as casual laws. Such a viewpoint breaks sharply with the old philosophy of classical determinism. Under the old science and philosophy we knew that reality consisted of time, space, and matter. We knew that matter could be hard and impenetrable, but we didn't know if there was something about matter that had a "soul."

Under the old science and philosophy any effect of the observer's mind or will on matter was denied. It was matter that changed thought and consciousness. Mind and matter were considered as two unrelated entities and consciousness was considered as a limited mechanism of the mind with little power to influence body or mind.

In the new age mind, matter, and self are related. Scientist such as Albert Einstein, have overthrown the idea of absolute time and absolute space and replaced it with the idea of relative time and relative space. Einstein proved that time and space can be defined only by reference to an observer or to a 'self' and his or her physical conditions.

Similarly, physicists Werner Heisenberg, Wolfgang Pauli, and Louis de Broglie were forced to overthrow the idea of certainty and the absolute nature of atoms in order to explain the nature of the atom and its swarm of atomic particles. Later, many other quantum physicists were forced to extend the same considerations to the swarm of quantum particles.

They also proved that the nature of the atomic and quantum domain can only be defined by reference to the observer or to a "self and his or her activities in setting up the instruments of observation. Quantum physicist, John Wheeler stated:

"The choice one makes about what one observes makes an irretrievable difference in what one finds. The observer is elevated from 'observer ' to 'participator'! What philosophy suggested in times past, the central feature of quantum mechanics tells us today with impressive force. In some strange sense this is a participatory universe." Thus, man and woman are unique because according to the theories of relativity and quantum physics, man or woman are the conscious observer in the relativity or quantum process; and the self has become exalted as the great participator in the cosmic process."

Similarly, Plotinus wrote in the second century: "There is in all of us a higher man or a higher woman that is more entirely of the celestial rank, almost a god, reproducing God. When the soul begins to mount, it comes not to something alien but to its very self. The self thus lifted, we are in the likeness of the Supreme".

In the lifting of the self there is a lifting of one's self-consciousness and understanding of one's identity. The light of self-consciousness lets us see the principle of love. Without love no society can meaningfully exist. Without order, no society can continue to progress. To lift the self is to achieve self-enlightenment which results in a balance between one's conscious mind with one's body. In self enlightenment, we realize that Nature has a Soul and we gain a biological and spiritual recognition of our individual wholeness and a recognition of our relationship with the expanding universe.

In this book, the lifting of the self is like a journey into the Universe on spirit wings. It uncovers thrilling new dimensions which enhance the idea of being human and enables one to say with Thoreau: "Read not the times, read the eternities."

It makes profound mysteries easy to understand and shows how they relate to the metaphysics of everyday life. It offers new illuminations for enhancement of the self and soul by presenting spiritual realizations.

This book is a song of praise for the vision and intuition provided by the keenest minds of men and women who have made known new wonders in the stars, the forces of nature, eternal truths, and the rhythms of existence. They have enabled the author to make a poetic and metaphysical presentation of the thinking of the self. This book hopes to inspire with prose and poetry as well as scientific fact. It brings to light many of the important poetic, philosophical, and spiritual ideas which can be related to astronomy, psychology, physics, biology, religion, and other fields. It adds a metaphysical dimension to our place in the universe and everyday life, elevates spiritual realization, and adds new dimensions to the category human.

Introduction

THE IMPORTANCE OF THE SELF

M uch of our everyday life seems to depend more and more on commitment to self and development of self-concepts. Such a commitment requires self-awareness, self-direction, and self-motivation and can lead to an increase in self-esteem, abilities and accomplishments. An increase in self commitment activity has occurred over the last two decades and can be seen by looking in the book called the *Social Science Register.* By comparing the 1975 volume with the latest volume, one can see that the former had two pages and 137 separate items prefixed with self-, but in the latest there are over 500 items prefixed with self. In the earlier volume, items prefixed by self were: acceptance, realization, confidence, criticism, image, interest, respect, sufficiency, understanding etc. In the later volume, are self-care health, self-consciousness, self-instructional training, and self-help literature.

Today, the good life, the good society, and even salvation depend on the proper preparation and presentation of one's self based on self help, self awareness, and self knowledge. The ancient Greeks said: "Know thyself." Today, we are reminded to "Do your own thing", "Be yourself", and "Find out who you are." Now, many people are searching for their "identity." People are enrolled in self type programs and are learning about themselves, diversity, and tolerance for other selves. All of us value diversity. We thrive on the widest range of possibilities to choose from. Our freedom makes the most sense when the presence of many choices exists.

To help us to achieve the self-type characteristic plus diversity, industry has invested in the notion of self and has brought us products that are: self-adjusting, self-alarming, self-cleaning, self-defrosting, self monitoring, etc. So now, we might say that Adam Smith's "invisible hand" is self-oriented! In addition, the national economy is referenced to individual persons, families, and firms. In this mode the equality of each individual or group is served by distributing scarce resources in a "market fashion." Self is affirmed in the creative work of industry in ordinary human affairs. A person or community should respond in faith, open mindedness, and gratitude to these tacit resources and structures upon which a sense of meaningfulness depends.

In their book *The Quantum Society*, Danah Zorah, and Ian Marshall wrote:

"The main challenge of our times is to link the inner world of the self with the outer world of society and to see both within the larger context of the natural world. To do so effectively, I believe we must come to appreciate the self, society, and nature all derive from a common source, that each is a necessary partner in some creative dialogue."

The self is important because if one knows their self, one has an enhanced sense of purpose and direction in action. As each person becomes more aware of their self, there is a spread of consciousness, an expansion of options, and greater vision in more persons. A society that knows itself has self-culture and is committed to moving toward a fuller realization of preferred values. It has the tools to transform itself, and is able to realize where limits need to be set to change for the better.

The self of each one of us has roots in the creative dialogue that takes place between us and Nature and the Cosmos. We ask what is the process of reality and what is the basis of transformation in ourselves, Nature, and the Cosmos- To answer such questions, mankind has in the past created myths which have added meaning to our inner world. Carl Jung stated:

"The need for mythic statements is satisfied when we frame a view of the world which adequately explains the meaning of human existence in the cosmos, a view which springs from our psychic wholeness, from the cooperation between consciousness and unconsciousness. Meaninglessness inhibits fullness of life and is therefore equivalent to illness. Meaningfulness makes a great many things endurable-perhaps everything. No science will ever replace myth, and a myth cannot be made out of any science. For it is not that "god" is a myth, but that myth is the revelation of a divine life in man and woman."

Today, the importance of myths, beliefs, and traditions have become devalued because of progress in science and industry. As a result, the meaning, devotion, and satisfaction associated with some myths, beliefs, and traditions has decreased. Some ideas and values no longer express the human condition with the power they once did. As a result, there is a danger that the nobleness of humanity may be scattered and ruined in favor of a world of complete unfaith where men and women have lost their selves and their Godhead. In ancient times the Neoplatonic philosopher, Plotinus wrote: "Man and woman are poised between the gods and the beasts;" but today, we might say: Man and woman are poised between God and the machines. Such an idea conflicts with the inward, unfathomable dignity of man and woman because we have a need for transcendence and inner development. They are a basic aspect of human nature.

The self is important because it takes part in transcendent and inner development and it encompasses or consists of the personality, persona and individuality. The principle of persona and individuality is the essence of man and woman. If we do not develop or distinguish our self, we set beyond our own nature and cease to be. However, man and woman are entering a new phase of existence. They have an increasing capacity to extend their freedom or to take away freedom from others. They have a new capacity to transform life or to accommodate it. They are removing barriers that were in the way of self-mastery, self-achieving, and social mastery. Class hierarchies and gender stereotypes have been reduced. However, there is still a constant challenge to develop a sense of self which enhances the quality of life. This is because on the other hand, each industrial type revolution has tended to decrease the importance of human values when in theory they were supposed to enhance them.

We have recently seen four industrial revolutions:

1. Replacing work done by hand with work done by machines.

2. Replacing hand operated controls with automatic controls.

3. Adding computer control of automation.

4. Adding robotics, information technology, and internet.

These revolutions offer us an opportunity to have a society that is the master of itself. Information systems and the internet increase mass education with worldwide and instant documentation of ideas and actions and result in doubled and quadrupled awareness of one person with another.

At the same time however, man and woman have lost some of their freedom to form their life and personality and have been forced to a appear as an "agglomeration of functions" to themselves and to others. For some this has resulted in a decrease of spiritual freedom and uniqueness. However, we know that man and woman are more than a collection of social functions or biological urges. We enjoy the many benefits of the Industrial Revolution and suffer from some of its drawbacks. Each Industrial Revolution in the past has built descending units of analysis and power. The Machine Age emphasized the need for isolated, separate, and interchangeable parts and this philosophy carried over to society to individual lives where relationships suffer conflicts and confrontation like "parts against parts".

The Industrial Revolution created an alienation among people by making them "factors of production," cut off from the natural world, society, and sometimes from their inner world. It viewed culture as through functions rather than through the individual person and overlooked the notion of self as socially constructed and differentiated.

As part of the Industrial Revolution, science tells us that the best way to grasp the meaning of an object is to know what class it is a member of. To know what an object is like, one has to search for its properties in a class. In this case, basic objects tend to lose their individuality, which is okay for simple objects but not for human beings. For man and woman this viewpoint must be vigilantly opposed. We must exercise scrupulous care to exercise common sense to protect the world of being human from contamination by concepts which are borrowed from another world, such as the scientific world, the machine world, or the computer world. There is a tendency to borrow from these worlds to replace the real with the abstract and introduce unauthentic existence. We must resist the impulse to order and classify human beings into fixed roles or rigid organizations where individuals are alienated from each other and the whole of society.

In addition to their vocation, man and woman needs to live creatively in meanings and spirituality. They need to reveal themselves in their soul and spirit in a successively deepening way. There is a need to connect human experience with meaningful, fulfilling beliefs in an intelligible manner. Anything which prevents being or spiritual self affirmation causes emptiness and meaninglessness. Anything which prevents an answer to, "What is the meaning of existence-" causes anxiety. Emptiness can be caused by the changing or vanishing of an object of one's devotion. In the modern age, many things which were once valued and loved, and even adored have lost their power to provide meaningful content. Some ideas and values no longer express the human condition with the power they originally had and there has been a loss of spiritual worth or self worth which threatens being. There is a fear that humankind has "strained or broken" its bond with the sacred. There is a fear that one may become a mere cogwheel in a technical apparatus and lose one's freedom, faith, and self-hood.

As a result, it is becoming increasingly evident that there is a need for something that will satisfy the inner nature of our human nature. English philosopher, Frederich Copleston, wrote:

"The human being is a unity, and if, as an individual, he or she requires society to satisfy his or her needs, he or she requires it as a person for "communication", to give or to overflow. The person is then a social being, and human society is, or should be, a society of persons." Society must satisfy the inner need of the individual and the person.

The individual and person are the two parts of what has been called the human unity. Emmanuel Mounier and the personalists philosophers have given their definition of the individual and person as follows: "Individual is used to denote man or woman as a center or spring of egotistic desire; the individual is the "diffusion of the person on the surface of his or her life and his or her satisfaction is losing themselves therein." The individual is the dissolution of person in matter. The individual is the man or woman who considers themselves as the only pebble on the beach." If the individual is not combined with person as a unity, it is a man or woman who has no moral vocation, no spiritual independence, no inner life of their own. They are a man or woman without a reason of existing.

A person, on the other hand, is connected to moral interest and is interested in "choice, conquest of self, formation, and mastery." Mounier defines person as follows:

"A person is a spiritual being constituted as such by a manner of subsistence and independence of being; it maintains this subsistence by its adhesion to a hierarchy of values, freely adopted, assimilated and lived, by a responsible self-commitment and by a constant conversion; it thus unifies all its activity in liberty and develops, moreover, by means of creative acts, its own unique vocation. "Philosopher, Denys de Rougemont also links together the person and vocation by stating that both are only possible in one being by a "unique act of obedience to the order of God which is called the love of neighbor…"

In the early part of the sixth century A.D., Boethius defined the person as "an individual substance of rational nature." St. Thomas Aquinas added the need for an embodied soul. Later, Descartes added the idea of a need for self-consciousness of the spiritual substance whose whole essence is to think. Later philosophers added emphasis on mind and spirit as a chief attribute of personality. For French thinker, Le Senne, the importance of self is related to personality because personality grows in the amount that the self apprehends or discovers value. He wrote:

"In the measure that value triumphs, conciousness personifies itself."

Personality gains as it realizes value, as it overcomes obstacles to the discovery of moral consciousness, and moral value, and free moral activity. It is moral value that makes man and woman stand out from nature's background.

Some philosophers have regarded freedom as the chief attribute of personality. Kierkegaard mentioned that a man or woman becomes an individual and person "by the exercise of their free choice, by freely giving form and direction to their life." French philosopher, M. Sartre said that "freedom is the being of man and woman." Christian philosopher, Gabriel

Marcel believed that personal freedom is "oriented towards others and to God: it is founded in Being and is oriented to Being."

The self is important because it is the most complete expression of our inner nature, our personality, our persona, our individuality, and our spirituality. The combining of the individual and the person in one human being was called by C.G. Jung as the psychological process of "individuation". "It is the process by which a person becomes a psychological 'individual' that is a separate, indivisible unity or 'whole'. It is the psychological process by which one's self embraces one's "innermost, last, and incomparable uniqueness to become one's own self. Jung called "coming to selfhood" or "self realization." In this process one "gathers the world to oneself." This process in itself points out again that the self is important for it combines individuality and persona.

The idea of individuality and persona was highlighted by the Greeks. Later in the Middle Ages, some began to view individual actions rather than collective actions, as the clear way to attain salvation. Shortly after, the Puritains started the belief that self-knowledge was necessary to properly combat sin.. This lead to the idea that a person was not just a mere part of a hierarchy, not just an observable and reportable person, but also a person with an important inner nature that was distinct from those previously mentioned.

As time went on, the importance of self has received increased attention in many academic and professional fields. Kant saw the dualist idea of self as subject and object, Descartes emphasized his cogito ergo sum, and Hume wrote of the relationship of self to consciousness. Today, the self is studied in many fields such as: philosophy, theology, sociology, anthropology, psychology, literature, art, music, and is being joined with ideas in quantum physics to construct better ideas of the self and society.

WHAT IS THE SELF

Today, in our modern world we can show how the interaction of chemicals or matter can be described with mathematical relationships but it is a mystery to show how consciousness originates in matter or from matter. Perhaps, some day there will be a unified theory of love, consciousness, and self that shows how mere molecules can produce self-realization or cosmic consciousness. It has been a mystery to understand the nature of what is known as the self, consciousness, the I, spirit, being, the ego, the id, and the soul. In this chapter, we will describe briefly each of these and show how each of these compares to what has been determined as different types on self, or self versus self.

In the *Book of the Vedas* of India one reads:

"In the midst of the sun is the light, in the midst of the light is the truth, and in the midst of the truth is the imperishable being." The imperishable being is the self.

Carl G. Jung wrote several descriptions of the self as follows:

"It is the central archetype; the archetype of order; the totality of the personality. It is symbolized by a circle, square, ring, child, or mandala.

The self is a quantity that is super-ordinate to the conscious ego. It embraces not only the conscious but also the unconscious psyche.

The self is our life's goal, for it is the most complete expression of the fateful combination we call individuality."

Some psychoanalysts have defined the self in still another way which shall follow. The reader may skip the next three pages if it seems too technical. Psychoanalysts have different ideas about what self is and I wish to relate four fundamental different descriptions. One might say that the correct description is all of the below.

1. Self is made up of the physical organism, every part of the psychological functions, and the social attributes. Under this general view, Hartman states that the ego is the equivalent of the self or idea of one's person.

2. Self is made up of mental self-presentation, which is contained in the ego and is developed by identifying with others. It may be developed consciously or outside of conscious awareness.

3. Self, according to Kohut is a super-ordinate, primary psychic constellation, the center of experience and initiative, and the main motivating energy (according to Curtis). This idea of the self, as well as items (1) and (2) above, fit the Western world cultural concept of self but not necessarily other cultures such as American Indian, Pakistani, Oceanic, Balinese, and others.

4. Self in non-Western cultures is different due to the collective unconscious and the ancient inherited experiences of each culture. Western Indians believe that the self is highly porous and fluid and changes by one's transactions in the world. Each culture does in fact produce a self which can be defined by a few key concepts if the culture is coherent and perceived as a timeless whole. There are cultures however, with inconsistencies and ongoing cultural arguments.

In some cultures, the self may be a "stripped away self" or an "altered self": which depends on accepting the standpoint of others (this may be called a developing self), or through dialogue a "shifting self". Nevertheless, there is an experience of wholeness and continuity associated with the self in other cultures. Scholars have tried to show how wholeness helps make sense out of inconsistencies in other cultures. Wallace and Fernandez point out that people in different cultures create all inclusive views of the world so that the self and total personality are coherently articulated.

Levis-Strauss made studies of totemism and primative classifications that show there is a tendency to coherent symbolic wholes which is a universal of human thought. However, fundamental cultural inconsistencies and contradictions are thought to be roadblocks to wholeness and unity of self. Fernandez states that wholeness in the face of inconsistencies is made possible by enactment of ritual which unleashes an argument of images that rest on metaphor and metonymy. This allows a return to wholeness by the process of iteration and the discovery of replication, and by the creation of novel semantic categories of wide classifications. It is conjectured that the use of metaphors and analogy allows "the collapse of separation into relatedness." Furthermore, Fernandez proposes that under stressful conditions, people turn to figurative language and the argument of images which bestow on them a better and more transcendent view of the world around them.

There are parallel psychological processes which people use to organize and interpret the sense of self. Some of these processes are condensation, displacement, transference, and identification. All of these processes depend on metaphor to combine experiences in an orderly way. They are as follows:

Condensation is the process of combining disparate thoughts into one image, especially when dreaming.

Displacement is when a person blocks out the memory of a bothersome experience by concentrating on a peripheral detail, which instead comes to represent the experience.

Transference is the combining of different experiences and having the image of one person absorbed into the image of another.

Identification is when a person becomes like someone else who means a lot psychologically to that person and develops the ego by "taking the role of the other."

All of the above psychoanalytical concepts are called semiotic processes because they make known to the psyche how to use 'metaphor and metonymy' to organize and internalize experiences that are interpersonal. By so doing, a person can construct a sense of wholeness and personal continuity from everyday life, even when life seems inconsistent and incoherent. All of the above concepts are helpful in organizing our memories. G.H. Mead stated: "We organize our memories upon the string of the self." We might add that the self is a string of memories. Memories help us to feel that we posses a coherent, continuous self.

Hallowell stated, "Human beings maintain awareness of self continuity and personal identity in time through the recall of experiences that are identified with the self-image." If you remember nothing of your personal experiences from yesterday, last month, or last year, you cannot maintain an awareness of self continuity in time. Therefore, memory is an important part of wholeness. However, a person with amnesia may not know who they are but they do know that they are and as such, they have selfhood. That is why self and memory are different. This is also the reason that we need to think of the self as different from self-identity and personal identity. Sir John Eccles and Daniel Robinson make the following distinctions: "The self and its unity arise from the irreducible awareness of being. One is aware that he or she is and knows directly that all his or her experiences, memories, thoughts, and desires inhere in this very self. Self-identity, however, refers to the knowledge one has of who he or she is and arises chiefly from memory. Thus, a given (amnesic) self can be lacking in self-identity.

Personal identity, on the other hand, refers to the knowledge others have of who a given person is. We may say for example that a total stranger has no personal identity (as far as we know) although be may well have self-identity. The totally amnesic person who is also a total stranger thus lacks both personal identity and self-identity but possesses self-hood nonetheless. Accordingly, such striking conditions as those popularized in The Three Faces of Eve pertain not to the existence of the three selves in one person but to three distinct self-identities possesses by one otherwise unique and "irreducible self".

The self is a beacon for directing behavior, for presenting desirable versions of one's image, for bringing together internalized views about who one is, and for depicting by metaphor the difficult to grasp abstractions believed to be there. In Western culture it is a metaphor which helps us to derive from our experiences the origin, nature, methods, and limits of our knowing so that we can add meaning to our sense of self.

Self is a relatively new term and concept but I believe that other previous writers were in their own way expressing what we could define as the self, today. Aristotle referred to it as a force which vivifies matter and directs it in its functioning. Hegel referred to a "plastic instinct," an unconscious purposive activity, bewusstiose zweckthaitkeit, which "acts without consciousness with a view to an end."

Masden stated: "It is a force which heals, regenerates, rejuvenates, harmonizes, and builds, and which brings us into that state of blessedness which we feel is the birthright of every human being." John Mueller described it as "organic force". Virchow labled it "inner necessity." Vageli had a longer word for it Verlollkommungsprincep or "tendency to progressive development." F.A. Long wrote of his Geschicte des Materialsmus or the mystical "domination of the part by the whole." Weismann mentioned it as "the constellations of energy." The neovitalists referred to the "vital principle." Frank Haddock mentioned it as that "majestic endowment." And, finally Emerson described it as "the spasm to swing the whole man or whole woman." All of these could be descriptions of what we refer to as the self- a driving force which can conquer fate, energize free will, power self direction, and increase spiritual nature.

The self is like a mystical supervisor that establishes values. Self is a formal power that fills one with enduring qualities by combining and storing experiences. Self is the invisible seer that is unseen.

One can say that I am my body or I am embodied because my body gives me orientation in the world and shapes how I perceive. The quality of one's body shapes the quality of one's perception. "What happens to one's body happens to one's consciousness." However, one's body does not help one to: understand deeper possibilities, balance emotions or instincts, or advance to a higher order of being. That can only be done through the self. Self can determine if there are spiritual dimension to human existence, can obtain insights into mysteries which transcend ordinary human knowledge. Only the self can establish the "motivations and intentions of the believing soul" by rationalization, systematic reflection, and by encoding layers and dimensions of meaning that need to be experienced. Only the self can elevate, illuminate, and give order to human experience.

At first glance, it might seem like the mind, ego, being, I, consciousness, and self are all the same thing. All of these are part of us and it would seem like we would understand all there is to know about them. Yet, when we try to explain what each one is, we wonder how something so familiar can be so hard to explain.

What we do know is that self is not mentality. Self is not perception because even one cell animals and protozoa have perception but not consciousness. It is speculated by some psychologists that caveman may have possessed thinking, reasoning, and learning skills without having possessed consciousness; and that consciousness was only possible after a critical mass of cortical brain tissue was produced through evolution.

Self is an analog of the real world. It is produced partly by vocabulary or lexical fields which are metaphors or examples of behavior in the physical world. Self is more of an operator than a physical thing. It is made up partly of volition and decision. We speak of the inner recesses of our mind, of our inner self, and our true self; and these are metaphors. The part of us that does the "seeing" is an important part of who we are.

First, there is our body which physically sees with its sense organs. This is the I of our body. Second, there is an analog I that develops in our mind what we see mentally. Third, there is the self whom is an object of consciousness.

It is natural to ask when does a living organism or entity start to have an awareness of its own awareness- How do unconscious, non-living atoms combine to form an entity that has conscious and self-conscious thought. What is it that brings awareness of surroundings and combines it with an awareness of one's self and identity- For some, the answer is simply that it is consciousness which is caused by some chemicals that flow around in the brain and that is the way it has been for mankind for 200,000 years. However, others believe that consciousness means having the ability to know. It has been suggested that consciousness is only possible if one has language or writing to use for communication; and that has only been possible for the most part since 3000 B.C..

Psychologist, Julian James, states that although our human ancestors had minds that were capable of sensing, perceiving, learning, and thinking, they did not have the ability to conceptualize a "me" or "I". In his view, consciousness requires three fundamentals: a mind-space, an analog "I", and narrating. These are essentials which are astounding biological achievements but mankind may have developed these not merely through passive biological evolution in the physical sense but in the evolution of the "mind's software" sense. The "mind's software" sense was evolved only after humans were able to produce symbols of writing, words, and language. The mind's software was not able to produce consciousness until this level was reached through culture such as the spoken language and written language. There has been little or no evolution of the brain anatomy, neurons, or chemicals in the last last thousands and thousands of years. However, it is believed that changes in the environment caused an evolution in political and social structures that resulted in individualism. This individualism was composed of three or more features:

1. Some men and women became aware of a distinct difference between themselves and their surroundings.

2. Certain people became aware of that awareness or of a feed back of information about oneself to oneself.

3. There was realization that the awareness belongs to oneself and to an "I"; and that there was a particular story to tell or history for this "I". There was a realization that there was an inner self, which was connected with the "I".

It was from these features that consciousness composed of a mind-space, analog I, and narratizing became manifest. Julian Jaynes gives us a brilliant example to explain what this means in the following explanation: "When a schoolboy or schoolgirl has a romantic day-dream about the person across the aisle they create a mind-space in which they and the other school kid are together. He or she with their analog "I: see into this mind-space. In seeing into this mind-space, they create4 a context- a kind of story- in which to embed what they see. This creating of a context is "narratizing"."

From this we can say with Jaynes that consciousness is "an analog I" narratizing in a mind-space." Mind-space is where introspection occurs. Thus, the analog "I" is part of consciousness, is "that which sees", is not a thing or process outside of consciousness, and is not the conscious experience itself. Instead, it "sees" all experience and is the molder or unifier of experience which passes on a unification of experiences to the self which has unified previous experiences. The self becomes modified by being receiving again new experience from the I"

Other development psychologists such as Daniel C. Dennett are in sympathy with the above view but emphasize that consciousness was brought about by conceptual changes within the brain rather than by biology. Dennett views the brain as the computer and the mind as the "software or the program" which contains the concepts. Before the spoken word or written word, people could not talk about morality or concepts so there was no morality or concepts from which consciousness could arise.

In terms of the "I", many things which one thinks are done by the "I" or self are actually done by the nervous system. They are done automatically without help from our "I" or inner self. They are done because of sense perception. But, sense perception is not consciousness. All life forms down to the algae and protozoa level have sense perception but not consciousness. On a similar basis, psychologists now know that consciousness is not all of mentality and that a lot of our actions do not require consciousness. Some psychologists believe that the "I", self, or consciousness are not necessary or even assist in learning. This fact has been proven in the classical Pavlovian conditioning studies.

It is worth describing how consciousness is different from the "I" and self. Consciousness is an analog of the actual world and is constructed in vocabulary whose terms are all metaphors of the world around us. It is not a thing but an operator like in mathematics. One of the main goals of consciousness is to "see things clearly." What does the "seeing" is an analog "I" which sees in mind-space a space used for introspecting and for locating time). In association with this, we hear metaphors like "fuzzy", "clear", "from my viewpoint", "do you see what I mean-" "they have seen the light", "it was clear to me", etc..

Self includes both consciousness and unconsciousness while the ego rests totally on consciousness. The self is perceived by both the conscious and unconscious but the ego is perceived only by the conscious. Ego itself contains memory data and an awareness of the body and is like a gate through which experiences of our outer and inner world must pass in order to be perceived. When motivation passes from our unconsciousness through our ego, we understand why we do something.

Unconscious activity includes all psychic activity which is not related to the ego directly. If our conscious mind is overdoing something at the expense of feeling, our unconscious mind will act to provide feeling in a balancing way, and may use dreams, fantasies, or images in literature, movies, or plays. Images and symbols of the unconscious are caves, bodies of water, or mazes, and enclosures. The process of becoming one's own self involves confronting the unconscious and its symbols. This is the process of becoming aware of one's uniqueness and identity apart from the collective of society while maintaining esteem for the collective norm. The ego is very important in this process because it receives symbols from the unconscious and makes them become conscious.

In addition, we must say that the self is not the "I" or consciousness. Self is the object of consciousness, not consciousness itself. Self changes through environment, time, culture, child development, and community and procedures self consciousness. Self-consciousness is conscious of its own consciousness or its own self. It is the result of two factors: the invention of writing which is empowers man and woman to "see" their thoughts-and two-changes which occurred in society in the political and business area which allowed a person to be an individual. These two factors interacted and produced self-consciousness.

In simple consciousness one is aware of things around them as well as one's body and limbs. In self consciousness, one is aware not only of plants, animals, one's own body, but of oneself as an entity apart from the rest of the world. It is through self-consciousness that one is able to recognize one's own emotions as objects of consciousness, is able to know what is true or false.

Richard Bucke wrote in his book, *Cosmic Consciousness*: "Self consciousness and language (are two in one, for they are two halves of the same thing) are the sine qua non of human social life, of manners, of institutions, of industries of all kinds, of all arts useful and fine."

The possession of self-consciousness and language (its other self) by man and woman creates an enormous gap between him/her and the highest creatures possessing simple consciousness (without an "I" or narrating-self). The self of man and woman alone can hear the voice of the oracle of Being, and can feel the marvel of what-is. Self exists outside or beyond all phenomena. This means that it is transcendental. Self moves through and unifies all phenomena it comes on contact with and unifies them into "experiences".

The self is the is-ness of Being, that what is of knowledge, the experience of Being in Nothing, the manifestation of consciousness suspended over a bottomless pit of atoms filled with the emptiness of space or Nothing. The self is like unformed matter which is powerful enough to form itself into being.

From the *IV Adhyaya, Brahmana of the Upanishads* we learn: "This eternal being that can never be proved, is to be perceived in one way only; it is spotless, beyond the ether, it is the unborn Self, great and eternal." This eternal being can be experienced in the silence of the soul.

One may ask, "Why do I need a self, an "I", a being, or self-consciousness- The reason is as follows: A tree in the field is given its existence. It does not have to struggle to be what it is, to define its identity, to define reality, to earn a living. Man and woman, on the other hand, are given existence but must define their reality. Thus, they must earn not only their living in but their reality in a metaphysical way, day after day.

And why is this so- It is so because our natural body and our natural being do not coincide. We are like a mythical character of the Ancient Greeks, a centaur. Our natural body is part of nature but our being is extra-natural so that we are partly existing in nature but partly transcending nature. Our natural body is with us from the day of our birth. It is not a problem because it is very easily realized. The Ancient Greeks had Athena and Ulysses as symbols to reflect the importance of the body. Our perspective of how we look is a major component of self-esteem. Body image often reflects the rest of our personality and induces a positive psychological outlook which carries into multiple activities. Today, we see that "lifting weights lifts spirits."

However, while the natural in us is easily realized, the extra-natural in us is not easily realized and this is why man and woman consider that the extra-natural is our true being. So here we have a case of self vs. self- the natural versus the extra-natural. One natural self is an entity whose character of being is made up of what it already is.

Our extra-natural self is not there from the beginning. It is an entity that is made up of not what already exists but rather what does not yet exists. We feel that our extra-natural self is our "true self" and we feel that we need to have a definite program and aspirations to give it meaning. And so, we set out to cause our self and realize that we must also determine what we are going to be. We find that imagination allows us to answer this question and be what we choose.

We them embark on life's journey to turn our imaginary intended to self into a real character but find that circumstances and experience requires us to forge a new extra-natural self and think out a new program of life. Everyday, we find there are choices to be made between A or B which will modify us in terms of A or B. As a result, we become a new self and become a product of our experiences. To become experienced is hopefully to become wise so that we may say with Shakespeare: "All places that the eye of heaven visits are to the wise man and wise woman happy ports and happy havens."

Experience allows us to invent our being and use our imagination. We must have imagination, because without it we cannot invent ourselves or determine what it is we are going to be. We must be free to choose whatever experience or identity we want; otherwise we will not be able to install the correct character that belongs to our real being. Experience shows us when our program of life to realize our self must be changed due to new obstacles or circumstances.

The new self is a new work of art and as Henry Miller wrote in, *The Wisdom of the Heart*:

"The new work of art does not consist of making a living or producing an object d'art or in self-therapy, but in finding a new soul. The new era is the era of spiritual creativity… and soul making."

This new era is a time in which man and woman go on accumulating self through "soul making". In the new era, the self is not in search of vain glory. It lives in view of the past and senses a oneness with Nature. If the new self could speak it would say with Chilean poet, Pablo Neruda:

"Earth give me back your pure gifts,
the towers of silence which rose
from the solemnity of their roots.
I want to go back to being what I have not been,
and learn to go back from such deeps
that amongst all natural things
I could live or not live; it does not matter
to be one more stone, the dark stone,
The pure stone which the river bears away."

These words recognize in the past of the Great, the Unique, and the Irreplaceable. One's new self can be judged in terms of the depths one reaches in making one's past origins one's own source.

There are numerous self versus selves in each of us. The self is like a multi faceted jewel. Each self is precious, and must be so for each is purchased at an infinite rate. Self is also pure like a jewel.

The Katha Upanishads state:

"As pure water poured into pure water remains pure,
So does the Self remain pure.
Know that the Self is the rider, and the body of the chariot,
That the intellect is the charioteer, and the mind the reins.
The senses say the wise, are the horses;
the roads they travel are the mazes of desire.
The wise call the Self the enjoyer when he/she
Is united with the body, the senses, and the mind."

The senses of the wise man and woman obeys the mind, the mind obeys the intellect, the intellect obeys the ego, and the ego obeys the self. Some psychologists such as Neisser believe that a person has five different selves corresponding to five different sources of self-knowledge. These five are as follows:

1. Ecological Self- It is the cause of changes in the position of one's limbs, of movements to a new environment, and changes of one's will.

2. Interpersonal Self- It sees and anticipates changes in facial expressions and behavior in others.

3. Extended Self- It constructs a personal identity on the basis of memory.

4. Private Self- It recognizes that its conscious experiences are its own.

5. Conceptual Self- It composes concepts about the self.

Neisser attributes these five selves to the self because he thinks that they are very different in the way they are structured and in the way that they originate. Furthermore, he thinks that there is a development history for each one which is different, that each can be subject to a different pathology, and that each makes a different contribution to human experience.

Another psychologists who believes that each person has a self is Frithof Bergmann. Bergmann believes that each person has a "true self," and that it is constructed by experiences on which meanings are attached that become psychological structures of a "true self" or a "false self". A false self is one that is thrust upon us that does not fit, or is one that has taken to heart too many "you should have done this" from too many people.

One might say that a "false self" is one which has separated itself from the source of meaning in the universe, from the creativity and "sixth sense" coming from within. It is very easy to let absolute necessities, goals, beliefs, and aspirations become dominant in life and overrule the swift subtle awareness of the body and the deeper meanings of nature and the universe. However, if this happens, creativity becomes blocked and the self becomes rigid. This is a common malady today because we have been forced to adapt to a mechanical sequential order of time.

In the earlier stages of civilization, man and woman operated within time orders that were based on custom, hunting, and rituals that were in accordance with the transformation of nature such as dawn, the new moon, the feast, the arrival of spring, the return of the sun, etc. These events are connected to an eternal rhythm in which change is related to an eternal reoccurence. In this eternal time order, people were bind together in a meaningful way instead of being isolated from each other. Human actions had more meaning and the idea of "being" was dominant over "becoming."

Around the time of Newton, there appeared a new concept of time that had a beginning and sequential order that moved into the future. It caused the consciousness of society to break away from the harmonies of nature and replaced the idea of an eternal rhythm or "eternal now" with a concept of always moving forward for the "better". Because of this, the idea of "becoming" became dominant over the idea of "being."

By accepting the new mechanical, sequential time order in place of the old time order of nature and the eternal, people tend to become cut off from the natural occurring, important, multifaceted cycles, rituals, the new moon, the change of the tides, and community.

In this case, the importance of earlier and eternal time orders fade into the background and the incessant order of mechanical succession dominates over the life's value, genuineness, and depth. This can cause a feeling of loss and a feeling of longing to feel something real in an intensive way to feel oneness and wholeness in a healing way or spiritual way with oneself, with community-in short to feel existence; to feel alive.

Albert Einstein himself was aware of this problem and wrote:

"A human being is part of the whole, called by us the Universe, a part limited in time and space. He or she experiences their thoughts and feelings as something separate from the rest- a kind of optical illusion of consciousness. This delusion is kind of a prison for us, restricting us to our personal desires and to affection for a few persons nearest to us. Our task must be to free ourselves from this prison by widening our circle of compassion to embrace all living creatures and the whole of nature in its beauty. Nobody is able to achieve this completely, but the striving for such achievement in itself is a part of liberation and foundation of security."

In addition, one could say one should also learn to enjoy the basic goodness or ordinary experiences of -your body, your self, your thoughts, your emotions, and feelings.

In addition to the explanations of self given above, psychologist explain the self in other ways. There is the Freudian self which is composed of the id, the ego, and the superego. The ego is like a peacemaker between the id (an oversexed and aggressive satyr or succubus) and the superego (a disapproving maiden aunt). However, it is said that the Id can keep secrets from the ego. The "I" does not have control over the Freudian self. Ego exercises control over the id through reason. If the ego represses the id too much, neurosis shall occur: whereas if the id is given total freedom, society shall be destroyed. Therefore, some believe like Machiavelli that a balance of power between government by force and by seduction is necessary to keep people under control. The self projects itself out into community in a sense of feeling and meaning that unites inner thoughts, interacts with others, and imprints some particular long lasting effect. Then, it is reflected back to itself.

The self that shares experience with community is projected from one's 100 billion brain neurons, 10,000 billion brain cells, 100,000 genes, and 600 million, million, million hemoglobin molecules. Hemoglobin molecules are springing into existence in one's body at the rate of 400 million, million per second and an equal number are being destroyed at the same rate. And each moment, each minute, man and woman have a new thought, mood, desire, and sensation that says "I am a new I."

The self dwells in two worlds-the outer world and the inner world. In each world the self meets the spirit but in different ways. The outer world is a "vale of soul making," where we live not in ourselves but become a portion of that around us.

"High mountains, waves, and sky are part of me and of my soul, as I of them." - Lord Byron

The self is a vale of world making where "high mountains are a feeling "where stars are the poetry of heaven;" where we see into the life of the thing. Some may call the vale sacred; some holy. For some the vale may be a plunge down. That which stirs in us is the world. The soul's awakening adventure is to meet the image of either a dying earth or an earth rising; to live in the depths in spiritless years; or to received the sacred, to create a being more intense than was endowed, to connect with inner wellsprings and outer soul scapes for information and inspiration.

For some of us an outer soulscape might be a personal project such as a sacred garden that is described by Elizabeth Murray in her book, *Cultivating Sacred Space*, or visiting some of her far away favorite soulscapes such as:

"Kokedera Temple in Kyoto, Japan; the l'Orangerie museum in the Tuillerie garden in Paris; the Rockefeller garden in Seal Harbor, Maine. There are also the vision quests worth exploring such as Delphi, Lascaux, Chaco Canyon, Grulin, Conneonara, the Black Hills, Kauai, Hawaii, Mount Fuji, and many others. These are some of the soulscapes of the world. Soulscapes are Nature's Wisdom.

Our lives are universally lengthened by experiencing the many soulscapes of the world. Soulscapes are the right hand of Nature. Nature has given us being, but soulscapes give us soul so that essence exceeds existence.

If the soul could have become aware of the eternal, the infinite, and the incomprehensive without soulscapes, soulscapes would never have been created. They enable the soul to have "free flight into the wordless."

RAISING SELF AND THINKING TO AN APOCALYPTIC PITCH

Thinking is the dressing up of ideas, is the shaping of the storm into a symbol of mankind's passion, is the forming of life's diverse gyrations into exciting living rhythms, is calling the weak and the strong to general consecration, is building a path to rainbows and sunsets. Thinking is looking at details beyond the big picture, is finding courage beyond fear, is picking up the pieces and creating a wholeness where none had existed.

Thinking allows us to say with Emerson:

> "I am the owner of the sphere
> Of the seven stars and the solar year,
> Of Caesar's hand, and Plato's brain,
> Of Lord Christ's heart, and Shakespeare's strain."

Thinking is a realization by the self of an inner sea of sensibility that connects the reason and understanding of our inner universe to the soul of the outer universe. Johann Tetens, a professor at the University of Copenhagen, wrote in 1977. "The self comes between, and creates new representations out of those already there, makes new points of union, new connections, and new series. The power of thought discovers new relationships, new similarities, new co-existences, and new dependencies… and makes in this manner new channels of communication among ideas."

Great thinking is the lifting up of transitory ideas to educate the spirit of the age. The poem, the play, the story carry us out of ourselves into a synthesizing experiences where we sense the interplay of words upon each other and we respond to clues, attitudes, and emotions. Out of new thoughts, feelings, and sensibilities we become new works of art. Dorothy Leigh Sayers wrote:

"Every work of creation is threefold; an earthy trinity to match the heavenly!

First, there is the Creative Idea, passionless, timeless, beholding the whole work complete at once…

Second, there is the Creative Energy begotten of that idea, working in time from the beginning to the end, with sweat and passion…

Third, there is the Creative Power, the meaning of the work and its response to the living soul.

And, these three are each one equally in itself the whole work."

In the creative thought there is the sacredness of origin, the holiness of originality, the dew of freshness, the priority of philosophical genius, and the capacity to extract knowledge with an intensity of feeling that no one else has done before. In great thinking there is often similarity. Shelly reminds us that, "There is a similarity between Homer and Hesoid, between Aeschylus and Euripides, between Virgil and Horace, between Dante and Petrarch, between Shakespeare and Fletcher, between Dryden and Pope. Each has a generic resemblance under which their specific distinctions are arranged." It is said there are elements of Homer and Virgil in Shakespeare. Great thinking lies not necessarily in completely original beginnings but in an exclamation of living experience that results in self-realization.

Geoffrey Hartman wrote that originality is "consciousness of self raised to an apocalyptic pitch." The self lets art, music, sculpture, music, literature, science, etc. Originate in a great leap. Colton said:

"If we can advance propositions both true and new,
these are our own by right of discovery;
and if we repeat what is old, more briefly
and brightly than others,
this becomes our own, by right of conquest."

Theodore Parker wrote, "Thought convinces, feelings persuade. If originality furnishes the fact with wings, feelings is the great stout muscle which plies them, and lifts them from the ground." Thought sees beauty, emotions feels it.

There is a need for the arts to supply man and woman with an alternative to the thinking that they encounter every day in a culture where mechanical substitutes and electronic fragments have replaced nature and spiritual satisfactions. Writers, artist, sculptors, and musicians can remove the crust from customary thinking and offer penetration into spiritual satisfaction. Rochefoucauld wrote: Penetration or discernment has an air of divination; it pleases our vanity more than any other quality of mind."

A writer can turn the sensual into "a superhighway to the soul's entropy" as Norman Mailer stated, or redeem the mind of man or woman. John Stuart Mill described the collective poems of William Wordsworth as a medicine for his state of mind because "they expressed not mere outward beauty, but states of feeling and of thought colored by feeling, under the excitement of beauty." Of Wordsworth's Collected Ballads, William Cullen Bryant said, "A thousand springs seemed to gush up at once in my heart, and the face of nature suddenly changed into a strange freshness and life." William Hale White said, "Wordsworth did for me unconsciously, what every religious reformer failed to do,- he created my Supreme Divinity." And, William James was pulled out of a spiritual crisis by reading Wordsworth's *Excursion* and by reading Renouvier's vindication of the freedom of will.

The idea of thinking and self has been manifested in sculpture and in fact it was a prevalent theme in the Renaissance. Donatello depicted the biblical David in a new Classical nude sculpture where David is not looking at the defeated Goliath but towards his own graceful, lean, muscular body as the instrument for his heroic deed, and appreciates the beauty, energy, and strength of his self. Later, Donatello depicts the self from almost an opposite viewpoint in his wooden sculpture of Mary Magdalene. In this case, the once beautiful body of Mary Magdalene is withered, and the body is repentant and virtuous after years of self-mortification. But, there is a beauty in the unity of the mind, body, and soul; and we can see the dignity and excellence of a woman without bodily beauty.

This reflected the theme of the Renaissance. Gianozzo Manetti, a humanist of the fifteenth century, wrote a book entitled On *The Dignity And Excellence of Man*, which was the theme of the painters and sculptors in Florence, Italy at that time.

The profound thought of the day was about human relationships and human destiny. Two examples were from Michelangelo and Raphael. Raphael painted the frescos in the Pope's Private Library. Michelangelo painted the Sistine Ceiling which is passionate assertion of the unity of man's body, mind, and spirit. Michelangelo also made a sculpture of David which was different from that of Donatello. This David is sternly watching for Goliath and the approaching army, and his face is tense, his sinews are tightened for battle gathering power, and muscles are coiled for battle. However, there is also something else. In the face of this David, one sees a spiritual force that the ancient world never knew. It is a heroic look that defies the blind forces of fate and exults the powers of mind and spirit of self to the utmost.

In conjunction with the above, we receive a confirmation from the words of Michelangelo himself when he wrote: "My eyes longing for beautiful things together with my soul longing for salvation have no other power to ascend to heaven than the contemplation of beautiful things."

In the contemplation of music we have a unique type of thinking. Ancient cultures considered the voice to be a link between the inner and outer psyches. The voice, music, and sound have been considered to be a source of balance and health for many people for many centuries. There is a mysticism in the music of the spheres. Carlyle wrote : "Who is there that, in logical words can express the effect that music has on us" Music helps us orchestrate a healthy mind, body and soul. The 4 1/2 beat is a basic rhythm which is found among civilized and uncivilized people all over the world. It causes the heart to go along with the beat and one experiences the inner self.

Rhythm has been referred to as the heartbeat of music and controls all relationships within a work of music.

Melody is the soul of music.

Melody is a series of tones that are significantly related so that one perceives a beginning, a middle, and an end. Just as words and sentences in a paragraph convey thought, so too, the tones in a melody have little meaning by themselves but are impressive in relation to one another when taken together. Music causes beta waves to move down the body and evokes a memory pattern in the body which results in a "new you". Music conveys an energy pattern that we receive by the mind body and limbic system in the midbrain.

Rhythm is a primal imprint in us. Sound is registered in the middle of the brain not the ear and causes a change in consciousness.

E. T. Hoffman wrote, "Music discloses to man and woman an unknown realm, a world in which he and she leaves behind them all definite feelings to surrender themselves to an inexpressible longing." Heine described music as, "a glimmering medium between mind and matter." Music is a kind of inarticulate, unfathomable speech which leads us to the edge of the infinite, and let's us for moments gaze into that. Schopenhauer, the philosopher, made a great observation when he said:

"Music is quite independent of the visible world, is absolutely ignorant of it, and could exist in a certain way if there were no other world."

The flow of music conveys an intellectual meaning or body of thought, just as all creative thought does. It is said that creativity is the very essence of reality and that it is not conditioned or limited by anything but itself. Creativity is the pure emergence of potential and formative energy out of the infinite universe. Associated with creative thinking may be synchronicities, epiphanies, illuminations, and mystical experiences where awareness fills the self and releases meaning, energy, and perception so it means that the self is released from the restraining order of time as creativity flows into consciousness.

It is believed that only creative thinking but thinking in general is derived from hierarchies of energy such as the quantum field, morphic field, plus the effect of what is known as the implicate and explicate order of the universe. We will briefly discuss what these are.

From the scientific point of view, it is believed that ever day events are the result of pure chance due to the fact that they are based on quantum processes. It is also believed that thinking may cause amplification of small effects of microscopic quantum processes and result in a "bias of the odds" which leads to a different outcome. Physicist Eugene Wigner has suggested that thinking can act at the quantum level in a process called "the collapse of the wave function" which results in a well defined order rather than chance state.

Biologists, C.H. Waddington suggested that living matter at the cellular level reacts to a field of information outside the cell that influences its formative process. Quantum theory suggests there is a basic oneness between the process of thinking and the universe. At the smallest units of nature basic building blocks appear as a complicated web of interconnections between the various parts of the whole.

In the same context, biologists Rupert Sheldrake has stated that there are morphogenetic fields of memory which are fields of information that exist for living and non-living matter. It is believed that a hierarchy of such fields directs the formation of living and non-living matter and its behavior. These fields are fields with account for identification and characteristic forms of organisms and other developing systems in their coming into being and which are evident in the embryo or development stage. It is recognized that these fields must have measurable physical effects in some way to be of scientific value and this has proven to be so.

The morphogenetic theory of fields states that particular morphogenetic fields are the cause of the distinguishing form, shape, and organization of systems at every level of complexity, whether it be in biology, chemistry, or physics. These fields provide order out of chaos for a system by influencing the events of the progress or emergence of a system in the face of an outcome that would otherwise have many possible probabilistic outcomes when considered from an energetic viewpoint for a physical process. By so doing, the fields order the events which in turns orders the system which results in a pattern. The morphogenetic fields themselves have a characteristic form, organization, or structure which they get from a previous similar ("ancestor") system; and this causes an accumulative effect which acts across space and time. "This causes complex, organic molecules or crystals, plants, or cells to take on a certain pattern because past representatives used that pattern. This is seen in shellfish with spiral shells that are mirror images of one another, or" left and right handed. "We see also" left and right" handed previous systems effect the morphic field to produce both "left and right handed" subsequent organisms.

At the germ of life, living things take on a polarity from light, electric currents, or chemical gradients. Such polarity shall be seen to have a direction from root to shoot in plants or head to tail in animals. The morphogenetic fields themselves do not have an intrinsic handedness associated with them but take on the same polarity and left or right handedness as the germ of life. It is also interesting that while amino acids and sugars can have a right of left handedness when seen in a test tube, that in living things it is always different. In living things, amino acids in proteins are left handed while most sugars are right handed and all of these are hardly if ever seen outside of living things or things which posses the morphogenetic fields.

As the size of a living system changes, the morphogenetic field associated with it becomes bigger or smaller. This may be the reason that I am the same person as an adult that I was as a child. My body and brain are altered in size and content but the essence of me has remained the same. Even though I live in a world that wants to mold me, there are a set of norms, steady states, potencies, and purposes of which I am composed and which will never change. I am not a mere set of repetitions, reflexes, or reactions.

I maintain my own identity and endure in spite of altered circumstances. No mere collection of matter or particles could do this. I have an organized pattern, a wholeness just like the universe, and an end seeking. I am a treasure house of possibilities, directives, and ideals that reach fruition in me as a person or a self that has developed potencies and tendencies. One may say that it is the self that "secretes" the body, soul, and personality like a clam secretes its shell.

It is seen that there are hierarchy of morphogenetic fields which are like fields within fields and that these correspond to the structures within structures of a body or organ. As an example in a plant there is an overall field, a field for the leaf, a field for the leaf's vascular differentiation, a field for the various small openings or minute orifices or slits in the epidermis of a leaf, and a field for the hair cells on the leaf. The latter are all lower level morphogenetic fields and they behave in a way which tends to be independent. The same is true in animals and humans. This idea has been proven by observing developing organisms which have been damaged and then repaired by grafting tissues taken from one region or another. As repair progresses, the primary embryonic morphogetenic fields lose the ability of overall regularization as numerous secondary morphogenetic fields begin to provide local regularization of the organism.

It is believed that the conscious self interacts with the motor fields of the body. The fields are associated with the physio-chemical states of the body. The self interacts with the motor fields but it is not the same as them, nor is it merely the same as the brain changes. It interacts with them but remains "superior to them". The self however, has properties of its own and cannot be simply defined in terms of matter, energy, morphogenetic fields, or motor fields. The reason is that it does not depend on only physical states but conscious states. This is why some people can be clairvoyant or perform parapsychology feats.

One may wonder how the self expresses its own properties through its own body and through the world at large through the motor fields. There are two ways. In one, the self selects between possible motor fields; in the second way, the self can also "cause" new motor fields such as insight and become a creative source itself. This is why the self also has the capacity to produce an indefinite number of sound patterns and phrases. The proof of this can easily be seen in the enormous development of an indefinite number of patterns and details in language, music, mathematics, science, sculpture, painting, writing, and computing. All of this involves the development of conceptual or creative thought by the conscious self, which is giving rise to new forms and new patterns by causing new motor fields.

It has been speculated that there could be a hierarchy of other creative agencies throughout the universe, which can cause motor fields or morphogenetic fields that these fields can interact with us, and that there is a unity with life that flows throughout from the earth to the universe and back.

Looking at the universe and thinking from a quantum structure or process level, there is a quantum phenomenon which reminds us of the morphogenetic field. It is called the Bose-Einstein condensate phenomenon because it was named after the Indian physicist Bose and Einstein because they first suggested that it existed. One description of this is that quantum force implies an attraction between photons. If there is a gas with a lot of identical particles, which have an integer spin like the photon, and if the gas is cooled down to a very low temperature and the movement of the particles is slowed down, then the attractive forces begin to dominate. This results in what is called a Bose-Einstein condensate of these particles. It has been experimentally observed.

The Bose-Einstein condensate is the most highly ordered phenomenon there is in the natural world. It has many parts that are unified within one another and in phase with one another so that their wave fronts overlap and they behave as a single whole identity. This phenomenon does not always require low temperature. A laser for example, is where many photons behave "identically" as one single photon and seem to make "choices" from many possibilities that could be. One may say that things that display Bode-Einstein condensate behavior also display a type of quantum unity and a type of quantum causation which is similar to unified thinking or consciousness and free will. They also display a continuous changing order and a high degree of unity so it is as if all the particles are acting in concert and so there is no interference between separate parts.

One may say that the ultimate stuff of the universe is thinking. It has several attractive features. It is connected with values, it has free will, and it has purpose. If one were to ask where does thinking come from- One could say that it comes from the brain, the central nervous system, which is composed of billions of cells called neurons, biological molecules, biochemistry, elementary particles, quantum particles, and forces and fields. These exhibit coherence, hidden order, inseparability, and subtle connectivity down to the quantum level. Thinking consists of visible quantum connections whose omnipresent influence is direct and immediate. This connection enables the mind to interact with the brain on a quantum level without violating the law of conservation of energy.

One might paraphrase the Buddha and say that thinking comes from a vast net woven of a countless variety of sparkling gems, each with numerous facets. Each gem has a reflection in itself of every other gem in the net, and is in oneness with every other gem.

In 1994, anaesthesiologist, Stuart Hameroff, of the University of Arizona was surprised to notice similarities between properties of thinking and quantum properties. He observed that,:

"The unitary sense of self resembles the properties of quantum coherence and nonlocality; non-deterministic free will resembles quantum indeterminacy; intuitive reasoning resembles quantum indeterminacy; intuitive reasoning resembles quantum computing; and differences and transitions between pre-, sub-, and non-conscious process resemble how, quantum possibilities become hard realities."

Rolf Landauer, an IBM physicist, has shown that from a quantum basis, there are in fact no theoretical minimum energy requirements for transmitting information. In addition, studies in quantum locality have shown information can be transported instantly by "quantum teleportation." And so, we may say that beneath the everyday world of human experience there is a connected world of intermingling possibilities which is a ground state from which fundamental and intermediate forms spring forth.

From the world of human experiences, religious, scientific, artistic, sociological, and musical models arise which are emotionally rich. Such models arise from the human experiences of healing, renewal, and new patterns of life and provide order and clarity in our lives. Models may be about relationships, patterns, or processes. Religious models express our experience of relating to God. Models are different from concepts or metaphors in that they offer more emotional clarity than concepts and are more precise in their comprehensive ordering than a concept or a metaphor; however, all are infused with value. One may say that the most underlying theme is that inside each man and woman, there is a good person struggling to emerge and that goodness and morality are due to the inner self rather than the problematic outer self.

In the doctrine of *The Vedas*, there is a connection between atman consciousness) and Brahman (the Supreme Self or World Consciousness). It is believed by some that transcendental and mystical states of being may be due to an individual connection to the Brahman consciousness. This could happen in the practice of yoga or meditation when the self flows into the fundamental state of unity with the rest of reality.

One could also say that when the individual pure ego (atman) flows into the universal ego (Brahman) there is a merging of a field of pure consciousness with a field of pure consciousness and that it produces a feeling of oneness with the universe or with God in a nonatomic reality that has a feeling of wholeness.

Similarly, Carl Jung proposed that there is a collective unconscious which is able to extend its influence to the external physical world. Quantum physicist, David Bohm, stated that thought is a system because to him the body, emotion, intellect, reflex, and artifact are one unbroken field of mutually informing thought. They are contained in each other to such an extent that they are a system. The system not only includes thoughts,'felts' and feelings, but it includes the state of the body: it includes the whole of society- as thought is passing back and forth between people in a process by which thought evolved from ancient times." Self is the complexity and depth of all this.

Thought is the partaking of itself as self. In addition, parapsychologist, G.N. M. Tyrxel proposed similarly that "people share regions of their minds at a deep unconscious level."

This was called the theory of subliminal selves which states that a person's mind has the attributes of both selfhood and otherness from self. It is believed that in this region of the mind telepathy and psychic powers are possible.

Several quantum physicists such as Niels Bohr, Arthur Eddington, Henry Margenau, Evan Squires, and Henry Stapp proposed that the individual mind connects with the individual brain by "influencing quantum processes within the brain."

The miracle of thinking and self consciousness is due to the action of chemical transmitters located in small membrane-bound sacs contained in the terminal branches of nerve fibers that end at sites where neurons make functional contact. One of the important aspects of the action of the chemical transmissions is that it does not violate the physics law of the conservation of energy. This is made possible by a quantum physics like process called exocytosis. This is a process where the above mentioned small membrane-bound sacs contained in the nerve fibers fuse with the terminal branches of nerve fibers that end at sites where neurons make functional contact and transmit ions.

The transmission from one neuron to another takes place by the "quantal emission" of 5,000 to 10,000 molecules from one neuron to another at a site of functional contact or site of transmitter release (a bouton). The space across which a bouton (or transmitter site) contacts another bouton is about 200 angstroms and is called a synaptic cleft. It has been determined that there are about 2,000 small membrane-bound neuron sacs in a bouton.

When a nerve impulse invades a bouton, it causes a secretion of thousands of calcium ions, and of these it takes only four of these calcium ions to cause the process known as exocytosis which is a quantal release mechanism.

These are several philosophers who deny the existence of a self but as parapsychologist Douglas Stokes said:

"There cannot be a stream of consciousness without a riverbed for it to flow through," and the riverbed is the self and soul.

The process of receiving nerve impulses is called dendrite. A grouping of the principal neurons of the cerebral cortex which do the receiving are called dendron and they are of pyramidal shape. The impulses generated by the experiences of the "I" are called psychons and they are received by the dendrons.

John Eccles stated, "There could be thousands of types of psychons, each with a matching type of dendron, the grand total being forty million psychons for an estimated forty million dendrons, of the human brain.

The transmission of molecules from one neuron to another takes place under the influence of a quantal probability field which alters the probability of emission from one neuron site to another. This quantal probability field does not contain energy or matter but is influenced by the thinking intentions of the individual. Intentions are non-material mental events such as the desire to do something.

To be associated with quantal probability, a typical representative collection of the small membrane bound neuron sacs must have a magnitude of mass which allows it to operate by the Heisenberg Uncertainty Principle. The quantum physicist, Henry Margenau, determined that the mass of the small membrane-bound sacs in a nerve terminal is 3 times ten to the minus 17 powergrams, has an uncertainty of position of 1 mn, and an uncertainty of velocity of 3.5 nm in 1 ms which is the correct order of magnitude. Even though there is no velocity or movement of the neuron sacs, it has been concluded that probabilistic emission from one neuron to another could be changed by a thought acting similar to a quantal probability field. It is believed that the probability field of a mental intention gets distributed across many, many neurons and changes the probability of the emissions of the neuron sacs.

There is a great amplification of the transmission between psychon and dendron because for each psychon there are 100,000 sites at which neurons make contact with each dendron and amplification is "several orders of magnitude". It is psychons that provide a unifying experience but it is psychon-dendron reciprocal action that generates our basic happenings and all on a quantum level as neuron membrane sacs secrete multi-molecular packets or quanta into the synaptic cleft as they fuse with nerve fiber ends of terminal branches. It is believed that there is a unique psychon for each unique experience and that each is connected to a specific dendron and that this produces the mind-brain interaction.

John Eccles notes that the ability to experience self-consciousness or self-awareness may be due to the fact that psychons may exist apart from dendrons in a unique psychon world of the self. If so, this would explain how we store all of our diverse experiences in life as a unique unification of thought from moment to moment.

The unique world of selves is the unique world of psychons, each individual with their own psychons. It may be that the great collection of psychons is what produces the unity of thought.

Similarly, Henry P. Stapp, a quantum physicist wrote an article called *"Quantum Propensities and the Brain-Mind Connection"* in the *Foundation of Physics* in which he stated:

"A conscious thought is a real thing that has an essential unity. It is not merely an aggregation of simpler parts. It is fundamentally one whole thing.

Nothing in classical physics can create something that is essentially more than an aggregation of its parts. But a quantum actual event does exactly that: it creates a single new actuality by grasping and combining together into a unified new ontological whole diverse aspects of the prior situation. The availability of integrative actual events of this kind is the first of two fundamental reasons why one must turn to quantum theory to achieve a rationally coherent understanding of the mind-brain connection: the reductionist classical-physics conception of nature is logically unsuited to the task of accommodating essentially unified conscious thoughts.

The second fundamental reason why we must turn to quantum theory is that classical physics has, as is well known, no rational place for consciousness: it is already logically complete... The physical world as it is conceived in classical physics, consist of nothing but the various particles and fields, whose properties are, within the theory, spelled out completely. There is no logical place within this conceptual structure for another kind of unity such as consciousness: if consciousness is put into the theory at all, then it must be put in simply 'by hand', rather than by virtue of the logical structure of the theory.

The logical situation in quantum theory is quite different: there is an absolute logical need for something else, such as consciousness."

UNITING SELF AND SPIRIT THROUGH PHILISOPHY

T o a philosopher, the questions that have been asked in philosophy are often as interesting as the answers that have been given. Philosophers have never lived in a vacuum; their writings have always been influenced by the writings of other philosophers, as well as by the society in which they live. It is often useful to study one philosopher in the light of some preceding philosophical writing of which he takes cognizance in his writings. For each period in history there is usually a certain interest which predominates in the writings which occur in the given period. In the time of the ancient Greeks, before the time of Socrates, there was a strong interest in knowing what the universe was composed of fundamentally. But with the philosophy of Socrates came a notable change in focus from man's environment to man himself, and his relation to other men.

In recent times, philosophers like Martin Heidegger, have emphasized that man and woman is a being that is preoccupied with or looking for "the other" in a forward movement toward the realization of his or her possibilities. Man and woman is a being that transcends himself or herself as they move forward toward the future. "My world" is one's world". One discovers themselves as a being within the world and as a being that is socially related to other beings. Man and woman are the shepherds or guardian of Being.

For professor of Philosophy, Frederick Copleston, man and woman can never be free from crowd-consciousness, however they can realize themselves apart from the crowd. These are two choices. They can be completely absorbed by crowd-consciousness, "thus gaining assurance at the expense of personal responsibility and resolute self-direction." But, this is "unauthentic existence". Or man and woman can in a reasonable manner take personal responsibility for their actions and future until death. This is "authentic existence."

To avoid being distracted from one self extensively in order to fulfill, responsibilities, which only you can fulfill, is "authentic existence". It does not mean one must withdraw completely from the world, as man and woman must always maintain contact with society.

Strictly speaking, in terms of the above definitions, authentic existence should only be practiced within limits. In response to this, one might remember the viewpoint of the philosopher, Hegel, that a person fulfills his or her true nature, not just as an atomic individual, but by accepting his or her moral responsibility as a member of society.

On a similar note, Karl Jaspers, a theistic existentialist, had the view that "I am the possibility of my own being, in the sense that I am never something already made, something finished and classifiable. I am constantly creating myself, as it were, or freely realizing my being through my choices." Existence for Jaspers is always possible existence. Perhaps more important is his idea that "My possibilities are not yours and my relationship to myself is not yours." Existence is something personal and individual. Furthermore, on a purely scientific basis, Being has no meaning. "Being or becoming is not a scientific question, it is a Transcendent question that arises as man and woman in the freedom of themselves and in the discovery of themselves move forward toward their true self.

Another philosopher and theologian, Rudolph Otto, wrote about how man and woman had an ultimate concern with that which "determines our being and non-being" and the meaning of life. Rudolph Otto laid the foundation for numinous consciousness by stating that it was directed by a "mysterium tremendum" or "wholly other." For Otto, the "truly mysterious" is beyond our apprehension and learning, not only because our intellect has certain irremovable limits; but because in it, we come upon something inherently "wholly other;" whose sense, category, and character are incommensurable with our own and before which we therefore recoil in an astonishment that strikes to the bone. The "wholly other" is something which is the opposite of ordinary experience, something, which seems to belong to another reality, something above the usual world order.

On a later note, for philosopher-theologian, Paul Tillich, life is the movement from potential being to actual being amidst a polarity between life and death. For Tillich, "Nothing can be of ultimate concern for us which does not have the power of threatening and saving our being… Man and woman is ultimately concerned about their being and meaning. Man and woman is infinitely concerned about the infinity which is their being." Man and woman's ultimate concern is to overcome self-estrangement and self-contradiction; and to realize salvation in self-reconciliation.

Similarly, love is a form of discovering the self in the other and discovering oneness of self and other in God. Self-transcendence is self-awareness. Freedom is found in self-transcendence. Man and woman are free when they they use conscious thought to "stand outside themselves" and "look at themselves". Thought, freedom, and self-transcendence are related. All help life to go beyond itself and become self-related. All of these activities are expressed culturally in different creative ways. However, for Tillich, freedom is a metaphysical "movement of separation" which is manifested in autonomy, individuality, or independence. All such activities can lead to "estrangement": and this is the tragedy of man and woman's life.

According to Tillich, relief from "estrangement" can only be obtained through man and woman's participation in God's eternal life. To be united with God is to gain the unlimited power to transcend the negative aspects of finitude.Both man and God are understood as self-transcendent. In prayer, one assumes the perspective of God and rises above one's finitude. Further revelations may be found in Tillich's three volumes, *Systematic Theology*.

Hegel states in two of his books, *History of Philosophy*, and *Phenomenology of Spirit*; that the goal of absolute knowledge is the reunion of the spirit with itself, or the self knowing the self, recognizing itself, making itself objective. The reunion of the spirit with itself is similar to a definition of beauty. Frederich Schiller described beauty as follows:

"Beauty unites freedom and supreme inner necessity in a harmony of laws not by inclusion of all realities but in the absolute inclusion of all realities." Professor of English and writer, M.H. Abrams, wrote that: "Beauty is also a middle state" which unites the "diametrically opposed" contraries of matter and form, passivity, and activity." One may say that then a brighter joy is then experienced through every image, every thought, and all impressions. Each of us has at least a certain amount of creative freedom in shaping the unification of our experiences into a progressive pattern and form.

Goethe expressed a similar idea and referred to it as an alchemy of nature. He stated:

"The two great drive wheels of nature are the concept of polarity and of enhancement. Every phenomenon must separate itself in order to manifest itself as a phenomenon, but "the separate seeks itself again" and if the separate first enhances itself it brings forth a new union of the enhanced parts a third, new, higher, totally unexpected thing."

Coleridge wrote of the "two counter-powers penetrating each other and generating a higher third which includes the former and the latter." Similarly, Hegel stated that: "the last stage of philosophy is the product of earlier philosophy, nothing is lost, all principles are pre-served."

We might say that the person who includes diversity in their life who combines the anima and animus who combines the fullness and existence with the highest sense of freedom and spirituality will draw the beauty of nature into themselves with all of its infinitude. Then, they will evolve into a new diverse unity which possesses a higher order of being and reality. This experience was called "the becoming of knowledge" by Hegel. Schelling wrote in *Transcendental Idealism* that nature is a poem that is encrypted. When we break the code, we find it saying the "self in seeking itself, flees itself." It achieves its goal finally when it returns completely to the self and recognizes that it is its own goal, its highest attainment, its own rejuvenation and feeling of unity.

ADVANCEMENT OF: SELF AND SOUL

The self is poetry in living form- a form that contains mystery, value, and resources beyond logic and reasoning. Advancement of self makes life brighter and brighter with each new day, and reveals to us simple truths, namely: that the plain is as valuable as the complex, and that which is above reason is not necessarily against reason.

Advancement of self is this: genuinely using one's intuitive process, sensitivity, and intellect to creatively realize one's own potential to appreciate mystery, and to appreciate the value of silence, joy, suffering, inner harmony, and meaningful moments of life within one-self and with others. In the simplest case, it means knowing that even if all else is lost, one's self is still a worthy self, and the potential for a good new life remains. In the most advanced case, it is when all of one's opinion seem to be written with sunbeams.

It is said that silence is the rest of the mind, and is to the spirit what sleep is to the body. Madame Guyon wrote, "Silence or rest from desires and passions is food, because it promotes quietness of spirit. But the best of all is silence from unnecessary and wandering thoughts, because that is essential to internal recollection, and because it lays a foundation for a proper reputation and for silence in other respects." Silence enables resolutions, effects sublime conquest, and magnifies latent power.

Advancement of self leads to wisdom with method, power with charity, and life with beneficence.

Advancement of self does not require psychoanalysis or confrontation of an ideal with the ego; however, one should be aware that an unresolved or unsolvable conflict could block self-realization.

Advancement of self should spring from one of one's motivators-such as aspirations, interests, or matters of necessity. We are born with aspiration rather than contentment. Longing and wishing flow from our hearts as flowers and trees burst forth from the buds of spring. We become what we truly and earnestly aspire to be by changing our mindset, and the mindset realizes itself.

A.P Stanley said: "There are glimpses of heaven in every act, thought, or word, that raises us above ourselves."

The realm of mystery adds enchantment to our pursuits. Motivation may come from necessity. Shakespeare wrote: "There is no virtue like necessity." Necessity is always the first motivator. Necessity that is combined with prudence is the source of moral progress in people and in nations. Necessity is the best instructor for it quickly arouses the human mind when doubt and hesitation disappear in the face of danger or passion.

Times of extreme necessity have produced great minds like a great lightning bolt is produced from the darkest storm. Even without necessity, we can process an interest that exalts us. It is always invigorating to have an avocation that seems as important as life itself. Exalted interest is known as enthusiasm, and is defined by the Greeks ad "God in us." The beauty and power of enthusiasm lie in its enlightenment of ourselves and others. It plans with audacity and acts with vigor. To experience that for which you had gladly hoped is a form of self-realization. One may attain physical or mental harmony, muscular development or attractive contouring, athletic, intellectual, or memory development. The main thing is that one has developed spiritually as a being-in other words, you are an important identity unto yourself. You are here not to crush others with prowess, but to help others with your abilities.

Self-realization manifests in using one's productive thoughts, feelings, and actions to reach a higher level of being oneself, living life fully in the "here and now." The effect of the self can be beautiful, and depends upon the emotional value and consciousness in which it exists. The idea of the self is one of the most unclear, most inclusive, and yet most influential of ideas. The self is composed of passions, recollections, truths, and waveforms that continually blend into each other.

To bring into focus the various facets of the self that can be unified, and to reject all other facets, raises us above the world, and simplifies needs. This vivid conception of the higher self results in the self-assertion of the soul.

The conscious attempt toward realization of the higher self is like a thirst, albeit with an intellectual extension that is practically and rationally interested in truth. Truth opposes and denies error, and thus is a vital part of one's being. W.M. Evarts wrote: "Truth is the gravitation principle of the universe."

Pascal stated; "There are two peculiarities in the truths of religion: a divine beauty which renders them lovely, and a holy majesty which makes them venerable; and there are two peculiarities in errors: an impiety which renders them horrible, and an impertinence which renders them ridiculous."

It is intellect that discovers intelligence in the universe, and the higher self is better able to see God in the world's works than is the lower self. Lack of truth does nothing but block out the light and destroy. It makes the world a moral wilderness, where no heavenly hand tends the seas and fields, Dispute, fear, and distraction emanate from the lower self. When it turns its thought inward, it finds doubt and ignorance, and is confused with questions. Darkness exists on every side. Lack of truth weakens conscience, will, love of neighbor, and the knowledge of the spiritual nature of being.

It is not the lower self that sees the beauty of heaven or hears the sweetest harmonies and rhythms of music; it is the higher self that nobly perceives all the bliss and glory of soul, nature, and intellectual perfection.The lower self is thus the "excuse" for the higher self's existence, just as truth is the "excuse" for the existence of ignorance. Truth most be combined with aesthetic and spiritual values to develop the higher self. By lifting one's self upwards from the merely factual and sensual, one's spiritual essence can etherealize the micro-consciousness and macro-consciousness of one's own soul and the soul of others.

We can get much of the truth we seek from science. Science and information systems now provide a vast amount of truth, but knowledge of science is not enough to develop the higher self-an acquaintance with religion of spirituality is also necessary. Our higher self thirsts not only for truth but also for eternal love and eternal life. Richter wrote: "Life, like the waters of the seas, freshens only when it ascends toward heaven."

When our higher self reaches for authentic power, and consciously moves through degrees of self-awareness, then strength and guidance flow into our personality and spirit.

In the book, *The Seat of the Soul*, Gary Zukav wrote: "If the personality that is tempted decides to align itself with love, clarity, understanding, and compassion, it gains power. Then the impulse toward anger, resentment, or vengeance loses power over it, and in this way-step-by-step, conscious-decision-by-conscious-decision-it becomes truly powerful."

There is a need to create harmony between our self and our experience. To experience beauty through our five senses, or mind, or spiritual self, is a way to attain harmony. It would be unattractive or unnatural for us to pursue truth, spiritually, and beauty if there were no happiness in such a pursuit. Beauty is a mysterious thing that is half discovered in nature and half created in our mind.

Bulwer wrote:

"Happiness and virtue rest upon each other, the best are not only the happiest, but the happiest are usually the best."

Hamilton stated:

"The happiest life is that which constantly exercises and educates the best in us."

Exercising a sense of truth, beauty, spirituality, great works, and goodness empowers the substantial riches of the mind, and bestows a dignity that is respected by the most petulant. Happiness, joy, ecstasy, rapture, delight, satisfaction, enchantment, peace, contentment, enjoyment, blessedness, and pleasure are precious and rare feelings with vibrant energies- energies that we need to receive in order to enhance our physical, intellectual, and spiritual response to life. Why is it that, when we see or hear a story that contains these feelings, and the story is about a lover, saint, artist, or mystic, it seems inspiring to us- It is because we are interested in the purpose of life, in personality, and in the nature and quality of personal life. We participate in the story and anticipate our own happiness by delightful expectations. As we exercise our sense of truth, beauty, and spirituality, we revealed the roots of our conscience and our preferences in human nature, and we compare transitory ideals that rest on singular conditions to ideals that are permanent and universal. We get a chance to experience intuitive and spiritual values above empirical and mundane values. Thinking about the basis of our own preferences has a good and purifying influence on us. We are able to consider excessive tolerance towards aberration of taste or morals, and we choose broader grounds for our own preferences and habits-resulting in greater awareness and more diversity in our aesthetic and spiritual enjoyment.

Poets, musicians, artists, writers, sculptors, and philosophers help us participate in aesthetic and spiritual experiences. They help us to feel the elusive and unfathomable emotions, dimensions, and ideals that exist in every mysterious thing. They offer us a clarifying effect on experience that, widens our capacity for observation, reacts well upon our powers, guides our attention, and increases the scope of our interests. They help us to cultivate our sensibility and progress to our higher self.

Cranch wrote:

"Thought is deeper than all speech; feelings deeper than all thought."

We all feel that we are deserving of a higher state of existence, also we delight in building airy bridges by which our souls win release from reality through expectation. Expectation is one of the joys of life which makes every blessing dear, and peace of the soul is the greatest expectation. Lessing wrote of this attitude in the imagined choice between the two hands of God, one containing truth, the other the endless striving for it. As an "Evolutionist" type sociologist, he chose the latter. The idea of progress beckons as a kind of salvation. It gives meaning to social programs and lends understanding to history.

There is more appeal in evolving than arriving. Following our inner desires aspirations, and thoughts, we allow ourselves to be dominated with the expectation that we will arrive at some fruition and fulfillment. We come into possession of our own thoughts; we become conscious of liberation and independence. We hope that evolving will mean the transition from poverty, profanity, and tyranny to wealth, spiritualism, and the life of freedom. Buddhism teaches that God's light dwells in the self and nowhere else: and this may be the reason that the mind of man and woman is striving to reach perfection through change.

In the 1973 version of the *Bhagavadgita*, Radhakrishnam wrote: "Any sense of satisfaction and security derived by submission to external authority is bought at the price of the integrity of the self. By developing our inner spiritual nature, we gain a new kind of relatedness to the world and grow into the freedom, where the integrity of self is not compromised. The sense of insufficiency, of barrenness and dust is due to the working of the Perfection, the mystery that lurks at the Creation. Wisdom is direct experience which occurs as soon as obstacles to its realization are removed."

However, personal change requires personal responsibility.

Wendel Phillips said:

"Responsibility educates."

It has been said that responsibility walks hand in hand with capacity and power. Responsibility gives vigor to virtue and tenacity to truth. It makes every hour lived the cultivator of a higher calling. The philosophical foundation of the universe is change. Theodore Parker stated:

"What is gained by one person is invested in all people, and is a permanent investment for all time."

But progress must be governed by moral and intellectual principles. If unlimited progress is allowed, that which is steadfast and durable will be destroyed, and the social life we all seek will be ruined. Good times are created when progress and limitations are balanced on an endless succession of ideas- ideas which build on the past but do not supersede it.

High aims and lofty purpose enable the self to change by arousing one's noblest and best efforts. High aims lead to the formation of high character.

Kant wrote:

"What are the aims which are at the same time duties- They are the perfecting of ourselves, and the happiness of others."

Aims are sometimes better achieved by tackling the chain of destiny one link at a time. George Santayana wrote about the liberation of self in his book. *The Sense of Beauty*:

"The aesthetic effort of objects is always due to the emotional value of the consciousness in which they exist. We merely attribute this value to the object by a projection, which is the basis of the apparent objectivity of beauty. Sometimes this value may be inherent in the process by which the object itself is perceived; then, we have sensuous and formal beauty. Sometimes the value may be due to the incipient formation of other ideas evoked by the perception of this object; then, we have beauty of expression. But among the ideas with which every object has relation there is one vaguest, most comprehensive, and most powerful one- namely, the idea of self. The impulses, memories, principles, and energies which we designate by that one word defy enumeration-indeed, they constantly fade and change into one another and whether the self is anything, everything, or nothing depends on the aspect of it which we momentarily fix, and especially on the definite object with which we contrast it."

HOW SYMBOLS ENHANCE MEANING FOR SELF AND SOCIETY

I n the field of sociology, the word person is used to rescue the individual from anonymity of collectivity, from being classified and grouped as a member of some material or organic phylum. Sociologists have prevented the concept of self from being robbed of any independent validity and from disappearing completely. Sociologists are helping to mold a self-guiding society of many voices, of a community that embraces many communities. They are helping individuals and cultures to come together in a vast diversity in order to build a better life.

In connection with this, knowledge of self has created a need for those we might call self-professionals. Their business is to provide knowledge about the self so that a person can socialize or correct their socialization habits. Such professionals include psychotherapist, psychiatrists, the clergy, teachers, and criminologists. They enable people to make a proper presentation of their self through advocating moral existence. They create dialogues so that we might accept others, and that we can have a central core of self-identity. It is through dialogue I learn to accept myself and discover whom I am and how to live from within myself towards another.

Self-professionals might be called developers of "self." Self is a product of development; it is not there at birth, it does not emerge full-blown overnight, and once established, it does not remain unchanging forever.

The concept of self matures slowly due to social experience. Sensitive and insightful determinations about the emergence of "consciousness of self" and the "social self" have been given to us by William Wundt (1916), William James (1950), Baldwin (1902), Thomas (1951), Charles Cooley (1902), George Mead (1934), Blumer (1969), Claude Levi Strauss (1959), Erving Goffman (1959) and Morris Rosenberg (1979). From them we have learned that personality and the self-concept is an important personality component and is fundamentally formed early in life, during childhood; but that fundamental changes take place in adolescence and even through adulthood. Subsequent developments and elaboration of the themes laid down by a person in childhood and adolescence take place over one's life span as the self-concept develops stability.

Each of has so to speak two selves. One is an open expressive revealed self, that is connected to the world. The other is a hidden, autonomous self that is separated from the world. The one self is open to the public and encompasses our physical demographic and behavioral characteristics. The other self is a private world of thoughts,feelings and wishes which is "barricaded" to keep the outside world from entering.

As we mature, we conceptualize the self more in the abstract and rely less on perception and more on conception to develop traits of self. Concepts are an intellectual manipulation of reality. Morris Rosenburg in *Concerning The Self,* wrote: "The concept selects, edits, highlights, and organizes reality in terms of a particular point of view."

Looking at the self in respect to the outer world and inner world we can say that both worlds are important to the self. The outer self encompasses the persona and ego. Persona is a protective skin or mask formed by the outer self. This system can be modified by the self to meet expectations by others or community. The inner self encompasses the animus (in woman), anima (in man), shadow, and repressed content.

To further explain our outer self let us compare it also to what Jakob von Uexkull called an Umwelt in his book, *Theoretical Biology.* An Umwelt is an enclosing world or part of ones "own world" which has meaning specifically for each creature and consists of only those objects or things in the outer world to which the creature responds. The idea of the Umwelt has been borrowed by the Existentialists philosophers, and they have added two new categories, the Gegenwelt, that is the world of society in which the individual lives, and the Eigenwelt, one's personal world.

Whenever man or woman studies new specialized knowledge, their Umwelt increases to encompasses a new classification of information. M. Ester Harding tells us of a dream in which: "the Umwelt was represented as a glass case or as a compartment shut in by a glass wall separating the individual from the surrounding world. This is a very apt image, for this Umwelt, this private world, is bounded by a transparent barrier separating one from the outside; like glass, it is also a reflecting surface on which one sees one's own image, while of course one thinks that what one sees is the outer world. Consequently, one judges everyone else by one's standard and from one's own standpoint. The universality of this condition is even reflected in the moral injunction to do unto others as you would say that they should do unto you. However, it is possible that the "other" would prefer something quite different from yourself."

Each person has an Umwelt that is formed by their own achievement, the achievements of society, and the environment. Language, myth, culture, art, and religion, are also part of our Umwelt. In addition, man and woman live in a world of hard facts, emotions, hopes, fears, illusions, disillusions, fantasies, and dreams. These things create opposing forces which intersect with our Umwelt at all times and force us to accept compromise rather than consensus as the best outcome. Stuart Hampshire stated:

"For the individual also, as for the society, compromise… is both the normal and the most desirable condition for the soul for a creature whose desires and emotions are often ambivalent and always in conflict with each other."

In addition, our feelings of self worth are often unduly dependent on the opinion, approval, or disapproval of others and this is part of our Umwelt that is outside of ourselves. In such cases, we are better for being praised but worse for being blamed. If we are convinced by others that we are no good, we can become a prisoner of rejection. We may feel a loss of reality with the world that we have been inserted into and it may be difficult to move forward into the future. However, we may say that our sense of dignity is connected to our use of freedom. Each of us wants to feel that there is something distinctive about us apart from others and that this is part of our identity. Each of us wants to feel that we are different in some special way. Each of us wants to know the difference and know that at least one other person knows this too. None of us wants to be passed by or forgotten.

As we grow older, we realize that others will forget us when we are not around. We are often too busy to think about even our most loved and closet friends and relatives. For many people there is a terror that their identity will no longer be confirmed and that after they die it will be forgotten. However, even though we must all die, not everyone will be rejected by others or have trouble knowing who they are. All of this goes to show that our sense of existence, our being, is dependent on other people's opinions and reactions toward us. In this sense, our entire self is outside of us.

If we look at the principle of the autonomy of life through the eyes of Uexkull, we find that for him life is an ultimate and self-dependent reality. He believed that there is an absolute reality of things which was different according to each living thing. Reality is immensely diversified, having as many different schemes and patterns as there are organisms. Every organism responds to it's own drummer, so to speak because it has an experience of its own. The phenomena that we find in the life of a grasshopper are not transferable to the life of a whale of course.

However, every organism is entirely fitted into its environment because it has an effector and receptor system. These two systems must maintain cooperation and equilibrium with one another or the organism or animal will perish. The receptor system receives outside stimuli, and the effector system by which it reacts to them are closely intermingled.

For man and woman the same principles hold true. However, man and woman have developed a third system which is a new characteristics and it is the distinctive feature of human life. It is the symbolic system. This system helps us adapt to our reality and adds a new dimension to our reality. It lets us think before responding to any stimulus. The symbolic system encompasses language, myth, art, religion, philosophy, sociology, and politics.

The symbolic system has caused myths, metaphors, and customs to become the motivator of our actions and has made cultural life more enriched and diversified. Sacred and non-secular symbols abound in our world side by side. By bringing the symbolic system into their Umwelt, man and woman no longer live in a merely physical universe, but a symbolic universe also. The symbolic universe contains opinions, fanciful dreams, illusions, and disillusions, imaginary emotions, art, and mythology. The symbolic universe is often more important than the physical universe to us. It is sometimes chaotic but it possesses a systematic or conceptual form. It contains conceptual, emotional, logical, scientific, and poetical language.

In the symbolic universe we experience the "luck of the draw" of who we are. In ancient Plato's times the myth of the formidable goddess of necessity, Ananke, governed the lots our souls selected. From Roman times into the Renaissance the myth called Fortuna accounted for an individual's individual character and destiny. In the modern age the principle called chaos in heredity is said to determine much of our destiny. However, this is only true to a certain extent because mankind has chosen to relate to the world in the form of symbols. By using symbols to derive meaning from the world, mankind has created a self-governing culture. Using symbols to define culture creates another large gap between humanity and the animals. Using symbols to define culture and the self creates an independent realm whose importance can only be understood in terms of the significance of the symbols. Sociologist, Marshall Sahlins stated:

"While the human world depends on the senses, and the whole panoply of organic characteristics supplied by biological evolution, its freedom from biology consists in just the capacity to give these their own sense.

The symbolic faculty 'defines' culture. This means that human beings are not socially defined by their organic qualities but in terms of symbolic attributes; and a symbol is precisely a meaningful value ... which cannot be determined by the physical properties to which it refers.

"It is a thing, the value or meaning of which, is bestowed upon it by those who use it. The meaning or value, of a symbol is in no instance derived from or determined by properties intrinsic to its physical form.

In other words, the meaning of the symbol is based on convention and not on the physical properties of the objects or the means through which it is presented. Thus, man and woman have patterned the physical world into symbolic terms, have given meaning to the symbolic processes. This creates the autonomy of culture through the use of symbols for language. The symbol is an arbitrary representation of "things" and shows that we are "cultural beings endowed with the capacity and the will to take a definite attitude toward the world and to lend it significance."

Our symbols point beyond themselves to another ground of meaning. Symbols are a kind of media of revelation which point to a reality that is sometimes different than themselves. Some symbols point to "ultimate reality". The power of a symbol can be heightened by comparing it with its polar opposite. This is seen when a symbol is taken from the finitude of this life but points beyond finitude, or negates finitude, or seems to point to a higher reality.

Paul Tillich stated that moral laws, divine commands, and final meanings are "symbols of being-itself or the ultimate reality," He believed that ultimate reality is comprehend as a result of revelation; and that revelation occurs when some concrete event, object, phrase, word, or relationship becomes recognized or "transparent" in its own importance. Such a revelation connects the search for meaning with being-itself, This may occur for example, in the comprehension of a moral imperative, in an aesthetic or entertaining significant experience, or in a recognition of significant meaning. When the "code" of a symbol is "broken" or recognized for what it is-then its true power is realized. Then the meaning of being is found not only in our concept of the symbol but through our "participation."

Symbols in general arouse emotions and change our perception of facts; therefore it may be better to promote short-term, practical goals without ideology and without deception. In the past, ideologists have used symbols to manifest themselves negatively as well as positively. In our everyday lives we see the clash of rival powers, politics, and their symbols. A symbol can only be destroyed by the power of another symbol.

Symbols are used as distinctive attributes in society to form personal identity and rational thought and their use marks us a different from all other creatures and as different from each other. The use of symbols is used to identify that a person is in a certain category. Symbols are used to generate specific social relations among people. The use of symbols varies so much that it is difficult to define a single idea of what it is to be human from a basic cultural 'humanness'stand-point that applies to all peoples.

In some cases, the symbol is treated as a "divine essence" and gives us a "sufficient likeness of all the things that are." Saint Augustine in *(De Trin. VI.10)* said:

"The perfect Word, not wanting in anything, is so to speak, the art of God."

A symbol can also be likened to the following quotation by *St.Thomas Aquinas, Sum. Theologica. 1.5.4. ST. Basil, De Spir. Sanct. XVIII 45*:

"The first perfection of a thing consists in its very form, from which it receives its species."

And also, (St. Thomas Acquinas, ib. 11129.2c):

"The form that is the perfection of the thing (its exemplary form) is the standard by which the actual form of the thing itself is judged: in other words, it is by their ideas that we know what things ought to be like *(ST. Augustine, DeTrin, IX.6,H)* and not by any observation or recollection of already existing things."

In creating symbolism, man and woman hold the world in their minds and form it into his and her image. In the modern period and post-modern period, symbols have become increasingly important, while the relative importance of objects has declined. This is because symbolic elements can be changed in form more easily than objects. Sociologist, Leslie White, observed that:

"It is the symbol which transforms an infant of Homo Sapiens into a human being. All human behavior consists of, or is dependent upon, the use of symbols. Human behavior is symbolic behavior; symbolic behavior is human behavior."

Since symbols can be recast more easily than objects, they are being used to recast society so that society can become self-guiding and self-oriented.

Support for this view comes from several sectors. There has been an expansion of education virtually everywhere in the world and it is enhanced by the use of the computer and internet, and television. More jobs require symbolic efforts than manual labor. In 1958, the United States become the first society to employ half its labor force in the services sector while less than half was employed in mining, agriculture, and manufacturing.

Today, much of the service sector can be called "The Knowledge Industry". This includes not only education, computers, information systems, but communications, telephone, printing, broadcasting, (and other forms of organized dissemination of symbols) and research and development. It was recognized by an economist that even as far back as 1958, the expenditure on knowledge was an incredible 29 per cent of the gross national product. Today, of course it is much more.

Today, educational leaders bring their knowledge to Washington and furnish symbols and advice to help committees decide help for social problems such as poverty, unemployment, birth rate, crime, and education. Their symbols and knowledge is broader and deeper than the bureaucrats and can help determine if a program is well or ill-conceived. At the same time, over the last decades the U.S. government has spent more on knowledge in total dollars and in percent of gross national product than on the other three "permanent" sectors combined-subsides to farmers, support to veterans, and foreign aid. Expenditures in the health field for knowledge has similarly increased. The number of research M.D. 's has grown more rapidly than the number of M.D. practitioners.

Symbols help individuals and groups make decisions about society. Symbols or knowledge, which is a set of symbols, perform two functions for groups and societies:

First, they provide a relation to the reality of a social and non-social environment.

Second, symbols (in conjunction with religion) provide "meaning" or connection for individuals and groups who are involved in receiving and evaluating incoming information, making decisions, and issuing directions to people who carry out tasks for a social group. Symbols or knowledge add options. Some alternatives are easy to implement, but vary in costs or consequences.

Meaning is achieved after facts are compared with group standards. A convergence of "collective and voluntary traditions" provides social guidance for decision makers. Society becomes "self-guiding" as its directions evaluate and exploitation of new points.

The modern world has become a construction of information and graphic images. Mundane and dramatic moments are not only formed by information, they depend on it. Symbols and information are altering the basic structure of experience. Instead of relying mainly on natural space, time, the seasons, and the link to other natural phenomena for basic experiences, we are relying on artificial realities which are created from relations and representations rather than from natural circumstances, contingencies, or the laws of nature. Our living spaces are furnished not only with objects but processes of the mind and symbols. We live by symbols, images, and pictures. We clothe ourselves in messages, e-mail, and broadcasts. We make all events communicable and sometimes forget that "symbolic behavior is human behavior."

For many, there is now a compelling urge to continually create a "new space" and a new content for experience. This is related to our search for meaning in life and our need to create fullness where there is emptiness.

In ancient times, symbols such as circles appeared throughout history and were according to Taoist an expression between the relationship of fullness and emptiness. It was often seen as a jade ring or earring and it also denoted "the tension between limit and possibility." It conditions awareness by our reflection on the symbol. The hole in the ring is emptiness while the band is fullness. Thus, the ring is the union of opposites-fullness and emptiness and it is a symbol of wholeness. The union of opposites which exist side by side in the ring symbolize the tension which exist between anima in man, and the animus in woman.

The ring is also called a mandala in Sanskrit. Mandalas are symbols which have appeared through out history and they are "symbols of unity and totality" according to C.G. Jung. A mandala is also a symbol of order. Furthermore, Jung stated that "mandalas are cryptograms concerning the state of the self a mandala also symbolizes the center. It is the exponent of all paths. It is the path to the center, to individuation.

"Symbolism" has also been discovered in the insect world by Norwegian nature photographer, Kjell Sandved. Kjell specializes in close up photography and has discovered subtle differences in wing design and color, even within the same species of butterflies. Sandved was hired by the Smithsonian Institution and has discovered and photographed the entire English alphabet spread out over the wings of the world's butterflies and moths. Sandved searched the United States and rain forests of the world before he found all the 26 alphabets in what should be called wings of wonder. Sandved's discoveries are reproduced in three different posters and in a book with the title *The Butterfly Alphabet*.

Some of Sandved's alphabets were discovered as follows:

- The letter "A" was discovered on the bird-wing butterfly from New Guinea.

- The letter "B" comes from the African atlas moth of Ghana.

- The letter "C" comes from the Christmas swallowtail butterfly of West Africa.

- The letter "D" was discovered on the small Apollo butterfly, which Sandved photographed in Switzerland.

- The letter "O" was discovered on the buckeye butterfly in Tennessee, which uses the "eyespot" pattern to frighten away predators.

- The letter "I" comes from a tiger swallowtail butterfly found in Tennessee.

- The letter "T" is found on the monarch butterfly which is found in Tennessee in the fall.

- The letter "P" comes from a tiger swallowtail butterfly found in Tennessee.

One might say that Nature has a soul now that we see that butterflies and moths "have" the alphabet.

Symbolism has been a fertile field of study this century for those such as anthropologist, Raymond Firth with his work on symbols, by religious historian, Mircea Eliade in his books about myths and symbolism, *Yoga, Immortality, and Freedom and Images and Symbols*, by psychologists,Carl G. Jung-*Memories, Dreams Reflections*, Italian Roberto Assagioli-*Psychosynthesis*,; by German Erich Fromm who relates psychological views to sociological views, by English sociologist and writer Jean Hardy who is a proponent of psychosynthesis: by professors of literature or art Beate Allert, Jeffrey Garrett, Richard Hardack, Karen Jacobs, Karl Menges, and Harald Wilnbock: by Spanish art historian, Juan E. Cirlot; and religious theorist Caroline W. Bynum.

Many writers tell us that symbols can have a transcendental side to them. Mircea Eliade relates a fascinating description in his book. *Yoga, Immortality, and Freedom*: "The "breaths," as we have seen, were identified with the cosmic winds and with cardinal points. Air "weaves" the universe, and breath "weaves" man-and woman and this symbolism of weaving developed in India into the grandiose concepts of the "life thread" and of fate as spun by certain goddesses. Confucian tradition teaches that Heaven is my father and Earth is my mother. It also teaches that Wholeness or Oneness is a feminine symbol and that it is greater than diversity.

Three religious theorists state that symbols give meaning to ordinary experience. Clifford Geertz tells us that symbols provide a cultural system in religion by creating a "model of" or a "model for" living. It shapes our ordinary experience and then imparts value from beyond it. It says that there are different things in our life that provide meaning. Paul Ricoeur believes that the meaning is already there but that the symbol names it and provides discovery by analogy. This viewpoint is important because it means that different genders may experience symbols in different ways as they mirror their reality.

Professor Caroline Bynum of Columbia University has explored the differences in the use and interpretations of symbols by men and women as they relate to social structure and social values. Bynum explains that religious symbols point men and women beyond their ordinary lives, and that religious symbols never prescribed or transcribe social status… Rather, they transmute it. Symbols that suggest maleness of femaleness-do not simply determine the self-awareness of men and women as gendered nor do they simply reflect cultural assumptions about what it is to be male or female.

Bynum tells us: "Gender related symbols, in their full complexity, may refer to gender in ways that affirm or reverse it, support it or question it, or they may, in their basic meaning, have little at all to do with male or female roles. Gender related symbols are sometimes "about values other than gender." For women a symbol may denote continuity or reconciliation; whereas for a man this may not be true. This leads us to ask, "Is it not possible to wonder what a symbol means without asking," For whom does it mean- Is it possible to attribute gender to Wholeness and Oneness that is beyond distinction or definition-" Is it possible to create a new society by giving new meaning to old symbols- Do men and women use the same symbols in different ways-

Geertz describes symbols as "historically created vehicles of reasoning, perception, feeling, and understanding." They give meaning to our lives by providing an image, allegory, text, or transformation of the world as it is and as it ought to be. A symbol "freezes" an image which would otherwise be lost to time and imparts value from beyond time. Assagioli stated that the symbol is based on analogy and is an important link that relates outer reality to inner reality.

Paul Ricoeur suggests that one's gender may change the experience of visualizing symbols. For anthropologist, Victor Turner, the symbol embodies a way of seeing not just a multiplicity of meanings but a multiplicity of relationships between meanings. Thus, to appropriate symbols is to appropriate meaning. One might say that a symbol is mysticism in the abstract. One might say that a symbol telescopes the important and complex events or characteristics of a culture. Symbols are formed by conceptions and abstractions which result from a unique cluster of meanings. Symbols embody or empower consciousness.

Carl Jung tells us in *Symbols of Transformation* "Symbols are not allegories and not signs: they are the images of contents which for the most part transcend consciousness." Mircea Eliade states in *Images and Symbols* that: "the symbol reveals certain aspects of reality, the deepest aspects, which defy any other means of knowledge."

Juan Cirlot tells us in his book, *Dictionary of Symbols*, that there is a list of symbols that are used very often around the world.

He relates their origin and meaning and states that "symbols link the instrumental with the spiritual, the human with the cosmic, the casual with the casual, disorder with order, and they guide us to the transcendental." He writes:

"The language of images and emotions is based upon a precise and crystallized means of expression, revealing transcendent truths, external to Man (cosmic order) as well as within him (thought, the moral order of) things, psychic evolution, the destiny of the soul) ... the essence of the symbol, is its ability to express simultaneously the various aspects (thesis and antithesis) of the idea it represents."

A symbol emphasizes our forms of knowing and helps us gain access to the truth so that we can absorb and retransmit the external world. Our form of knowing by the human body has evolved into a single organ, the eye, which brings about the coherence of all organic forms. The eye enables us to make a final determination about the fundamental unity of nature and bring about a metamorphosis of the self. Emerson thought of the eye as a rudimentary organ, that is nothing but one that absorbs and represents all. He wrote: "When I am uplifted into infinite space-all mean egotism vanishes. I become a transparent eyeball. I am nothing; I see all the currents of the Universal Being circulate through me; I am part and parcel of God." Here the self is united with God and the eye replaces the self.

From Goethe and Emerson we are told that "The first principles of nature begin in the eye of a leaf and the eye of mankind and end in the circles of the universe." The "governed" circle is the representation of universal order and galactic unity which enable every atom to donate its part to gravity and every photon to contribute to the light. Emerson emphasized repeatedly that "the universe is transparent; the light of higher laws than its own, shines through it."

When the eye surveys the world, by perceiving, representing, amd recognizing all of the objects in its field, the mind is not so much receiving reality as much as it is constructing reality. "It is the eye which makes the horizon. There is at the surface infinite variety of things; at the center there is simplicity of cause." When the form of an object is reflected in our eye, we share the aspiration of higher things to display a delicate projection of their essence.

Such constructions have brought us to a new society so to speak for some time. Some eminent Western biologists have stated that mankind's biological evolution has come to a halt and that society now is only evolving culturally. Biological evolution has been completely replaced by social evolution. There has been a "sharp break" or discontinuity in mankind's evolution. It has been "replaced" by the development of the human symbolic faculty and cultural transmission. This "new talent" of mankind transforms the whole of human life. As compared to all life on earth, mankind lives not only in a broader reality; it has now entered into a new dimension of reality-symbolism.

As such, mankind itself has introduced a new reality into the universe. Mankind is no longer just an oral culture but a visual, symbolic culture involved in diverse processes of image cognition and an inexhaustible capacity for inner and outer imaging. Society now uses images and text to transform and translate the memory it touches. Texts are visual phenomena that are to be deciphered and translated. Beate Allert explains, to translate is to illuminate, is to break the frame of meaning, is to "disturb momentarily the continuum of time, and to shatter the surface." Mankind now has a "science of thresholds" which enable multiple translations of many images into texts and texts into images. Such translations contribute to cultural change and involve all disciplines of study and every aspect of human life.

Barbara Stafford in her book *Body Criticism* states that the twenty first century will bring the "inescapable universalization of vision." Johann Gottlieb Fichte wrote: "We must not start from Being but from vision… Being is seeing that does not penetrate itself." In conjunction with this, one could say that poetry is seeing in the form of words that elevate the vision of man and woman beyond themselves. German philosopher, Schiften Novalis, tells us that poetry is the "representation of the unpresentable" He writes:

"The sense of poetry has much in common with mysticism. It is the sense of the unique, personal, unknown, secret, which needs to be revealed and which will need to be necessarily fulfilled. It represents the unrepresentable."

The priority of Being and our yearning for the Absolute cannot find satisfaction in ordinary thought, so it must seek fulfillment in the representative infinitude of poetry and art. It is because ordinary thought is based on conceptual finitude that such thought is limited. It is thus necessary to make a transition to aesthetics and symbols because they posses infinite variables and possibilities. Aesthetics is based on the idea of an "encompassing synthesizing visual world of symbols we project our enthusiastic vision. We extend our spirits and fill "the gaps of human life with light." We see "the secrets of the far" the spirits are reflected in "the bounty of life." Our aesthetic vision joins philosophy with poetry, science with art. Paul Ricoeur stated that symbols are part of a pre-given phenomena where our "consciousness surges into a present activity in a world already there."

Meister Eckhart wrote: "To be properly expressed, a thing must proceed from within, moved by its form." Art is the embodiment of a preconceived form. The characters in which art is written are called symbols. Symbols are the universal language of art. When we look at symbols that are of an ordered form such as art, sculpture, writing, film, photography, or architecture, we make connections with a reality that consist of colors, lines, mass, test, or textures. The content of symbols is metaphysical. In other words it has a meaning over and above the immediate value of the substance or object of which it composed. From such symbols, we become familiar with the aesthetic order and we can feel the Nature has a Soul and this gives us a feeling of oneness with a rational and spiritual whole.. Then, we might ask with Williams Blake:" Is there any portion of eternity that is too great for the eye of man or woman- Is participation in any part of the sublime too much a strain.

We can say that religious and aesthetic symbols are like Plato's Muses they are given to us "that we may use them intellectually not as a source or irrational pleasure but as an aid to the revolution of the soul within us, (of which a harmony was lost at birth), and to help us in restoring it to order and consent with the Self," In symbolism there is for the artist and the patron an ultimate spiritual significance of overall work of art. And in fact, the practice of art has been considered a rite as well as a profession.

Emerson tells us in his essay, *History:*

"Some men and women classify objects by color and size and others by accidents of appearances, others by intrinsic likeness, or by relation of cause and effect. The progress of the intellect is to the clearer vision of cases, which neglects surface differences. To the poet, to the philosopher, to all the saints, all things are friendly, and sacred, all events profitable, all days holy, all men divine. For the eye is fastened on life, and slights the circumstances, every chemical substance, every plant, every animal in its growth, teaches the unity of cause, the variety of appearance."

A symbol can be an "illuminated phenomenon" that offers a significance beyond itself. A symbol may offer signals of essential discovery or "moments of privilege" which "convert the very pulses of the air into revelations." Walter Prater wrote in *The Renaissance*: "Every moment some form… some tone … some mood … grows more perfect for that moment only," and to maintain a stream of such intense moments is "success in life."

Intense moments can also bestow intuitions of the self, inspiration, revelation, something suddenly visible or audible with clarity and exactness. When we read a book that is outstanding, we enter into a new world and recognize the truth of its fact and feeling. Similarly, when we see the subject of a painting or sculpture that is created by more than one artist we obtain a different view of what is real and of value.

"To make the primordial truth intelligible, to make the unheard audible, to enunciate the primordial word, to represent the archetype, such is the task of art, or it is not art." Artistic symbols help us recognize the aesthetic meaning of the universe in color, lines, sound, text, and material consistencies. Artistic symbols furnish us with intense moments, a formal relation with reality, and an aesthetic order of meaning and belonging to a rational and spiritual whole. A symbol may help one's "spiritual eye" adjusts to "an exact focus." Writer, James Joyce, in *Stephen Hero* referred to "intense moments" as "moments of epiphany" and he believed that it was the responsibility of the man or woman of letters to record the delicate and "evanescent of moments." One might say that an epiphany is a sudden spiritual manifestation of when "the soul of the commonest object ... seems to us radiant." The "moment of epiphany" is accompanied by the "freshness of transformation of ourselves."

SELF, SYMBOLS, AND THE FUTURE

A s the use of symbols accelerates through the use of computers and internet, minds are being fused with a "DNA of information." On the information highway symbols are beamed around the world as weightless bits. The future is being changed so that human behavior is not only symbolic behavior it is digital behavior. Every product and service that is eligible will be rendered digital. As this happens, the state of Being will be measured in a new way in terms of digital bit. A bit is a colorless, weightless, "digital atom" of shorts. It is the smallest element of the "DNA" of the digital information world. A bit state of being is on or off, true or false, black or white, one or zero.

In the digital world symbolism is greatly increased in the form of binary vocabulary to encompass information beyond numbers, letters, and words. Information such as audio and video is turned into digital "DNA." The digital process removes bits which are redundant or repetitious while using other bits for error correction. There are also new bits which state what the other bits are doing. They are called header bits.

Symbols, information, and bits can now be delivered to you in a way that creates a new experience. Symbols and bits can be filtered, sorted, prioritized, managed, prepared and delivered to you from newspapers, television, computers, and the internet right to your home or work. Information is compressed and condensed to save you time and costs.

In the world outside of the digital world, an object, form, or event is itself. In the digital world all things are embodiments of the real thing. Digital devices present intelligence on such a high level that the physical interface is unnoticed. Hopefully, they will never replace the conscious good looks, speech, gestures, expressions, and tone of voice which are presented by the real thing.

There is a big difference when communicating with a digital device than another real person or group. When a person appears before other people, he or she knowingly and unwittingly projects a definition of the situation, of which a conception of himself or herself is an important part. Listeners tend to accept the self projected an projected by an individual as a reasonable representation of his or her social position. Occasionally, an individual will intentionally present their selves in a particular way because the traditional make up of the group or social status require it. Others in the group will project themselves and respond to the situation under review.

When a person defines a situation, they make an implicit or explicit claim on others in the group as to what they are supposed to see. For a woman this may be even more so. Simone de Beauvoir wrote:

"Even if each woman dresses in conformity with her status, a game is being played: artifice, like art, belongs to the realm of the imaginary. It is not only the brassiere, hair-dye, make-up disguise, body and face; but that the least sophisticated of women, once she is "dressed," does not only present herself to observation; she is, like the picture or the statue or the actress on the stage, an agent through whom is suggested someone not there-that is the character she represents, but is not. It is this identification with something unreal, fixed, perfect as the heroine in a novel, as a portrait or a bust, that gratifies her. She strives to identify herself with this figure and thus to seem to herself to be stabilized, justified in her splendor."

For a woman and for man, the body expresses a vital energy which brings us into contact with others, an energy which seems to create and transform reality. Our culture of the body emphasizes the body as a symbol and instrument of communication. The body is a profound form of communication in interpersonal relationships (especially love) and not a dark realm of the instincts.\

Cultural sociologist and clinical psychologist, Alberto Melucci tells as:

"The body is, finally, for each of us the personal realm, the field of that specific awareness which distinguishes us from others.

The return to the body fuels our search for identity: our body is the secret place for with only we possess the key of access and where we may return to confirm our experience that we exist as individuals. The body is our unique and unalienable possession which gives us the power of self-recognition in an age when other forms of identification break down. No one else can tell us what we feel within our bodies: only we can express ourselves through the body."

The body is our underpinning to finding meaning as individuals. It is a symbolically loaded phenomenon that can deliver a supercharged flow of messages. Messages from the body are to be listened to, interpreted, and answered. The body communicates by its public display and by personally directed signals. We need new meanings to come to terms with everyday life and an attractive body furnishes sustaining experiences. Interpersonal processes can convey a deep-lying link of the within and without between two people. The challenge is to control the continuity and discontinuity of communication.

HOW ART INSPIRES THE SELF AND SOUL

A rt is like the soul. Both aspire to relate to all experience and both draw their composition from the whole of life. Each has to deal with segments of experience. To the extent that the life of the soul has form, it is a work of art; and the extent that society has an established order and form, it is a work of art.

The self goes beyond life when it combines form and intelligence and transforms formless matter and chaos into a desirable state we call art. Artists, writers, sculptors, musicians, poets, craftsmen, dancers, architects, and film-makers bring out from experience something that is significant, surprising, original, pleasurable, arresting, or exciting. They take us away from the unpleasantness, ugliness, and boredom of life to a different reality. In art related activities, such as painting, writing, music, and poetry we enter into an umwelt that is vast and metaphysical where our selves can function freely and find peace.

If society was ideally ordered, all work would have the character of art, and entertainment would involve aesthetics, appreciation and the search for the appreciation of life might be in an aesthetic experience.

The artist, sculptor, architect, musician, composer, dancer, writer, and poet are inspired by self belief and an imaginative touching of passions rather than just reason. Philosopher, Irving Edman wrote:" The things in a painting have more purity and precision and intensity than the things as seen by the routine practical eye. The characters in a novel have more urgency and clarity than the people we brush against in our hurried daily contacts." A picture by Monet of golden flowers may for the first time give us a true feeling of the reality of flowers. Anna Karenia of the novel by the same name may become more real to us than dozens of women of our acquaintance.

The artist, writer, composer, sculptor and architect does not find but creates a unity among things that are visibly or audibly separated or unrelated that lets us savor life or endure it. This may be why art lasts longer than figureheads. Dobson wrote:

> "All passes. Art alone Enduring stays to us.
> The bust outlasts the throne, The coin, Tiberius."

Artist, writers, composers, and sculptors see more clearly and vividly than most mortal eyes can see. They help us realize something outstanding behind the obscurities, something that fills us with energy, wisdom, and awakens what William Blake called the "Real Self" or Imagination. It is only in the contemplation of art, music, literature, poetry, dance, sculpture, architecture, and soul scapes that our restless mind finds peace. Matthew Arnold stated that the only way to remove the vices that affect the upper, middle, and lower classes of society is by exposing them to culture so that they learn what to value in life. Art, sculpture, music, poetry and literature create meaning out of personal experience and often claim our best moments.

It is part of our nature to be metaphysical because we often reason by analogy or symbolism. Our metaphysical nature seeks things that are on a higher than empirical level of reference. Our metaphysical nature seeks unveiling of things rather than disclosure. The study of sculpture or example should unveil and enlarge feelings not merely confirm them. An example of this is given in Nicholas Peusner's description of Michelangelo's sculptures in the tombs in Medici Chapel as follows:

"The question has often been asked what made him keep the untreated stone below his reclining figures of *Day and Night and Morning and Evening*. The answer is that he wanted them to appear in the act of coming to life out of a stony subhuman existence." This sculpture shows by symbolism the image of man and woman is completely unveiled when it is released from the dark forces of poverty and subhuman existence.

In a similar way, Paul Klee emphasized the idea that we should turn our attention from subject matter to content when he said:

"Art does not reproduce the visible; rather, it makes visible." The work of art is not just about the object or subject but what it makes visible or unveils about, feeling, the expression of intensity, meaning and mood.

Art, music, literature, and sculpture create a connection between the metaphysical world in which self knows all, and the physical world in which the self can never know all perfectly. The connection is made up of visual or audible symbols in which as Goethe said. "The particular stands for the general, revealing momentarily the unknowable." Essence is realized in visualization and unveiling. Juan Cirlot wrote, "The psychological mechanism that transforms energy is the symbol."

Tantric thought states that the world was created as energy then became more complex as it evolved into sound, then light, then matter, then man and woman. Ravi Kumar wrote in *Tantric Art*:

"Tantric Indian thought holds that each and every shape, color, object, and action in the world is a visible form of a vibrational level of a primal thought that exists beyond the sensate mind." Mike and Nancy Samuels wrote in *The Mind's Eyes*:

"These visible forms of vibrational levels, like symbols, are capable of infinite combination and rearrangement, giving rise to the innumerable nuances of knowledge."

Thus, art, sculpture, music, ballet, opera, literature, and poetry connect all magnitudes and patterns of the physical and metaphysical world. These things are a world in themselves. The arts, music, literature, poetry, and dance are in possession of Being and Visualization.

As nature is devalued and destroyed, these things become more important. Some have said that only these things can save us from the devaluation of all of Nature and the devaluation of all of Society.

The presence of diversity and flexibility in culture creates a potential for change, which is a key characteristic for survival. Nature avoids monotypes because they tend toward weakness and cannot produce anything new, and having little flexibility are easily destroyed. Art, music, poetry, and dance provide us with our own metaphors of life which we can fit to our own personality. Mary Bateson stated that:" We have our own mythology, our own possibilities to live out; and we are each our own central metaphor." That is what makes us and a diverse society strong.

The society that is different than the assembly line, that possesses flexibility and different viewpoints is empowered to change itself yet preserve individual ways of life. Cultural anthropologist, William Bateson, believed that variation comes from within rather than from the outside action of the environment and that it is seen in the primacy of form and pattern over matter which is the result of aesthetic sensibility of inner purity and intuition.

In variation, the artist, sculptor, poet, writer, composer, musician, and dancer select their themes and arrange them in a pattern and form to suit their conceptions of value and this results in coherence of meaning and a set of ordered values.

Joyce Cary explains in *Art and Reality:*

"All great artist have a theme, an idea of life profoundly felt and founded in some personal and compelling experience. This theme then finds confirmation and development in new intuition. The development of the great writer is the development of his or her theme- the theme is part of him or her and has become the cast of his or her mind and character."

In most cultures, the theme of the artist is driven by a need to express beliefs and aspirations. The demand for an artist's work depends on the extent to which the work shows creative force and ability to fuse invention and innovation.

However, an artist, writer, dancer, or musician selects a set of ordered values for their work of art and then creates an arrangement of the order to suit his or her conception, inspiration, and theme. With their arrangement, the artist, writer, dancer, or, musician conveys to us the character and the soul of the universe. They convey to us an intuition about the universal order of things in the deepest sense. An artist, writer, sculptor, or musician creates a path of discovery for us which starts in sensuous reality and leads us to the unexpected nature of truth and its consequences.

They offer a purely sensuous and emotional aspect of experience. They do not usually appeal to the practical or critical judgment except as it is concerned with technical achievement. They excite, they stimulate, and they give that intuition of the world of values which often have a direct effect on moral judgment and moral action; but they do not deal with that judgment and that action as a subject matter. That is why music, sculpture, architecture, and painting are called pure arts.

On the other hand, novelists not only deal with moral action they create it and are concerned with motives and morality from beginning to end.

Artist show us how to comprehend life through the senses and show us what the world is like in a way that science or words could never describe. An artist or sculptor helps, us visualize symbols, self, and the world from a particular mood, and from a certain character so that we feel a certain attitude toward something because of its shape, form, space, light, shadow, and color. Artist, Virginia Cobb, for example reveals in her book, *Discovering The Inner Eye*:

"Working with the simplified shapes created by the shadows on the walls of the canyon near where I lived, I learned to abstract my view, to search for most important elements of my form, and to define the textures and patterns nature has imprinted there. The series of rock paintings I did at this time is an example of how one simplified element-a rock-can suggest the larger forms of the landscape."

An artist unveils the uniqueness of life and delivers it to the immediacy of the senses and emotions. An artist starts with visualization rather than Being because intuition is not clouded by intellect. Art alone can code perceptual qualities into a sensory contact with life. Art is a movement toward one's inner self. Ralph Waldo Emerson wrote:

"The movement toward spirituality and one's inner self is a movement toward excellence by our comprehending faculties." For artist, Virginia Cobb:

"Painting is a journey. It is the way I mark my way through life."

Similarly, artist Ben Shahn stated:

"Artistic creativity is a movement toward spirituality. The moving toward one's inner self is a long pilgrimage for a painter. It offers many temporary successes and high points, but there is the residuum of incomplete realization which impels him or her on toward the more inadequate image."

Emerson stated:

"What lies behind us and what lies before us are tiny matters compared, compared to what lies within us."

In a like manner, Ben Shahn wrote:

"In the arts, particularly painting and poetry, the self is content… it is perhaps object and subject in one image."

Content is that, which we take for a theme or object, transformed by our self and creativity into feeling and meaning. Henri Matise explained that drawing is "not an exercise of particular dexterity but above all a means of expressing intimate feelings and moods." Sylvan Barnet states in his book, *A Short Guide to Writing About Art*, that the content of art is "conveyed in the language of art" such as by "short, choppy, angular lines, and gentle curves or by "thin, broken, agitated, nervous, or bold lines: or by vigorous or agitated brush strokes on a rough or smooth surface."

One of the greatest triumphs in life is to express the content of self by exercising one's own energies. Virginia Cob stated:

"When we are children we do not doubt the reality of our images, but as we grow in experience, we become so influenced by what others consider "acceptable" that we tend to lose confidence and allow others to determine for us what is beautiful or credible or real. As adults, it takes courage to believe in our own images, our sense of the real, which is the content of our work." It takes courage also not to invest our creative energies in an unbalanced way in the goals and aspirations of others. Robert Louis Stevenson reminds us that:

"To know what you prefer instead of humbly saying Amen to what the world tells you, you ought to prefer, is to have kept your soul alive."

ENRICHMENT OF THE SELF AND SOUL BY THE SACRED

There is, today, a real need to, establish or support that which is sacred. Modern media and science have weakened and eroded religious claims and have created a vacuum in some places. As a result, some previously held sacred claims now appear illusory due to humanization and rationalization. In addition, some religious philosophers have eliminated value out of being while others have eliminated value out of becoming. A transcendental philosophy which has a positive value for being and becoming is offered in the idea of the sacred self.

The sacred is associated with relative goodness and absolute goodness, and is the starting point for a reason, aesthetics, and morality. The sacred is the substance of being and becoming. Finite existence is sacred because of self- consciousness. Infinite existence is absolutely sacred because of absolute self-consciousness.

To ignore the sacred is to be profane. On the other hand, those that recognize the sacred are raised to their highest level and often discover love as a positive ingredient for existence. Sacredness is manifested in ethics, aesthetics, and community; and not in another world. Ethics is used in fulfilling becoming possibilities and spirituality possibilities. The sacred helps the individual and community to support one another in attaining their fulfillment by evoking both to pour out goodness to one another.

Spirituality acts in fulfilling by focusing the self on the absolutely sacred and by making the self aware of itself and achieving new depths of sacredness. One might say that redemption is coming to the sacred to reflect the brightest beams of divine glory. It is an individual experience because no one can attain enlightenment for another. The philosopher, Alfred North Whitehead, wrote that the quest for the ideal values of life "is what the individual does with his or her solitariness" and that religion "is the art and theory of the internal life of man and woman."

Mircea Eliade, a famous religious historian and researcher, stated in his book, *Patterns in Comparative Religion,* that," A religious phenomenon will only be recognized as such if it is grasped at its own level, that is to say, if it is studied as something religious. To try to grasp the essence of such a phenomenon by means of physiology, psychology, sociology, economics, linguistics, art, or any other study s false; it misses the one unique and irreducible element in it--- the element of the sacred.

The sacred is transcendent and converts ordinary objects, acts, and words into a series of transcendent variations and experiences. A sacred experience is often not reducible to reason alone or to some level of human experiences. Sacredness is like consciousness blazing into revelation, is like supernatural light filling the self, is like non-temporal realm of being which is attracting grace.

A sacred moment was described by Blake as a, "Moment that Satan cannot find." Goethe's poem, *Vermachtnis (Testament)*, mentions the "Moment of finding the center". Hoderlin refers to it as "the moment in which the imperishable is present in us" and the unfettered self forgets its sorrow and servitude. Rousseau said, "It is the supreme felicity, in which time means nothing" and "the present last forever, yet without indicating its duration and without any trace of successiveness"; and so long as this state endures one is sufficient unto themselves, like God."

The sacred is irreducible and will not be erased by humanization or rationalization. Redemption may be termed as coming to the sacred. Stephen B. Murray stated in the book *Toward a Metaphysics of The Sacred,* that:

"Spirituality springs from moments of sacredness, from existence catching itself aware of itself, of an awareness of identity of a self over against a self, of freedom and other characteristics belonging to "existential." Self-consciousness. It is in this realm of consciousness that religious language develops. The substance and meaning of religious language emerges and grows as the mind gives shape and form to its new height, depth, or quality of awareness."

Religion is not about some other world but this world experienced in a particular way. It is concerned with what is ultimately real the absolutely holy, the real basis, ground, or content of existence.

The meaningfulness or accuracy of religious language is dependent on the honesty and openness of the "observer" towards reality at the religious level of existence. There are no instruments of manipulation here for scientific experimentation because, at least according to many witnesses, at this level, the self finds itself confronted by a self. One is addressed or addresses the other. Religion is thus the superstructure for the soul's innermost prayer. It is a cathedral built on holy ground.

The sacred is accepted as the holy ground for unity. Only the sacred can mediate and make recompense for sin, for blind, insensitive destruction, mockery, and hate. The pain of existence consists in its very sacredness. If it were not sacred, there would be no grief. The sting of death is removed by profound gratefulness for the gift of self-conscious existence.

The German poet, Hoderlin, mentioned in the Preface to his book *Hyperion*, that we should strive for a unity "that ends that eternal conflict between our self and the world, to restore the peace that passes all understanding, to unite ourselves with nature so as to form one endless whole."

The sacred is irreducible and will not be erased by humanization or rationalization. We wish to add that which is sacred is distinct and set apart from the ordinary; and is experienced in prophecy, meditation, worship, persons, place, and natural phenomena that have long-lasting positive, uplifting influences on thinking, feeling, and acting. The highest limit of thinking, acting, and feeling consist of knowledge, of self-conscious existence and absolute existence. The lowest level of knowledge is the lack of self-consciousness.

There are three ways in which the self may interact with self-conscious existence. First, the self may change its mind about the object of enlightenment. Second, both self and object may reciprocate in the language of the spirit, so that, both are enlightened in the knowing process. Third, the self may stay the same but affect the object of knowledge so that it is seen in its components. The first may be called aesthetic, the second conative, and the third analytical.

These three aspects of knowledge form a class of signals and symbols in which the laws and regularities of existence are made into a language of self-conscious meaning, so as to satisfy the critical and practical intelligence of man and woman in trying to understand the qualities, power, and structural components of finite and absolute existence.

Aesthetics Way-The way of aesthetics is the most basic response to existence for it invokes sacredness for the beauty of existence. In this case, the self's idea and feelings are altered so that the object may be itself; causing the object to the perceived in its wholeness by interaction of the whole self.

Conative Way-In this way, the self has a feeling of the dread awe, and power of existence that fills the mind with blank wonder and invokes astonishment for the tremendous majesty of a divine nature. In conative knowing there is an interaction of the self with the object; and knowledge is gained about the power relationship which may lead the self to utter dependency on sacred reality.

Humanity often tries to make its desires or needs comply with an idea of the sacred, which is manifest in "the structure of the universe, structure of society, or a revelation from God. "There is a submission of the self to a higher existent Being with the thought "if it is the will of the Almighty."

Those who submit to the dependency on the absolutely sacred ask for things they need. The conative way thus become an important path for achieving goals by submission to a sacred reality.

Analytical Way- The Analytical Way invokes the sacred for knowledge or the principles of the wisdom of existence. This way is often associated with the great traditions of the East, Hinduism, Buddism, Taosim, and Confucianism. Self-conscious reason concentrates on a self examination of the structure of existence. Self is not changed and attempts to be detached.

The inner structure of self is related to a wider order of existence. Buddhism involves a very deep realization of oneself and the world. Hinduism has a similar practice known as jnana yoga ("knowledge discipline"). Its goal is to perceive the true nature of things. One who "sees" has achieved the necessary wisdom to be liberated.

Similarly, in the West, study is so highly thought of that it is a religious obligation. This is shown by the many schools and colleges where study is of the utmost importance.

There is however, a difference in emphasis of knowledge in the East versus the West. In the East, there is a major concern with the understanding of one's true self. In the West, there is a major concern with the understanding of sacred books.

Stephen Murray wrote, "Self-conscious reason consists of the self examining the structure of form of existence. The self knows by analyzing an entity into its parts. The object is changed but not the subject. The self is not changed in that it attempts to be detached. Reason synthetically relates the inner structure of the entity (the analysis) to the wider order of existence. It discovers the logic, inner order, or integrity of an existent as well as its structure of relationships with external entities. The form of the entity is logically described in terms of an "independent measure or classification system. Reason builds up a set of principles, law, or regularities that apply to existence.

Knowledge of existence is, however, more than the sum gained by feeling, willing and reasoning. Knowledge is fundamentally a matter of meaning and interpretation of existence that incorporates feeling, willing, and rational knowledge. Symbols are created that communicate holistic meaning. Sacred symbols are those found to communicate meaning intrinsically."

Sacred symbols give meaning to ordinary existence. In a discussion on the nature of sacred symbols Clifford Geertz stated in his now classic essay, *Religion As A Cultural System,*" that such symbols are "historically created vehicles of reasoning, perception, feeling, and understanding," which give significance to being and becoming by presenting a model of the world as it is and a model of the world as it ought to be. Sacred symbols are like blueprints that shape finite existence by reflecting it and in the process generate value from beyond it. They give rise to thought according to the area, class, district, or standard that are viewed as subjective. As such, there may be a multiplicity of meanings potentially, but each person will fit each symbol to their own particular purpose, occasion, person, or event."

For some, sacred symbols provide an orientation toward heaven, infinite reality, or the absolute and assure a connection with the same, so that life should not be lived in chaos. Some of the best examples of this may be seen among native or indigenous people all around the world.

The following is a native poem, which conveys the idea of sacredness:

"Then I was standing on the highest mountain of them all, and round about beneath me was the whole hoop of the world. And while I stood there I saw more than I can tell and I understood more than I saw; for I was seeing in a sacred manner the shapes of all things in the spirit, and the shape of all shapes as they must live together like one being. And I saw the sacred hoop of my people was one of the many hoops that made the circle, wide as daylight and as starlight, and in the center grew one mighty flowering tree to shelter all the children of one mother and one father. And I saw that it was holy... But anywhere is the center of the world."

Black Elk Ogala Sioux (1863-1950)

In the sacred self there is more in time than time, more in ourselves than ourselves. That which is sacred acts on all levels of human existence and integrates them into one transcendent intention. It animates the various strengths and variations of meaning of any sacred or religious outlook and lets one be moved by currents of sacred significance while maintaining an open-mindedness.

Rudolph Otto, A German religious philosopher, in his book, *The Idea of the Holy*, recommended that we form a "penetrative imaginative sympathy with what passes in the other person's mind. Then, we shall learn what is in their heart."

C.J Arthur, a professor of theology and religious studies at the University of Wales, gives us a perfect example of this in his book review of William Golding's novel, *The Inheritors*. Golding's book is about a confrontation between a small group of Neanderthal men and a larger group of Cro-Magnon men (supposedly the first homo sapiens). The CroMagnons have fled their homeland because of a dispute and end up in the Neanderthal's territory. Golding immerses us in a remarkable primitive religiousness in the mind of the other person.

Arthur tells us how the reader must see the world as it appears to its inhabitants while still maintaining the status of the observer. He relates that "Golding does not merely describe the Neanderthals from the outside, as an anthropologist would do. He attempts to enter the consciousness, to experience existence as they experienced it." He conveys to the readers mind sparks of primal innocence and resonance of sympathy and introspection. Golding "deprives himself of all analysis by himself or his characters in order to express the Neanderthal point of view. Incidentally, it has been established scientifically apart from this book that Neanderthal's skull did not posses a voice tract which was capable of making a, i, or u sounds. The vowel sounds are an encoding mechanism by which we humans can transmit information at a high rate.

Cro-Magnons were the first to have words, language, and perhaps a self. This story is a way for us to explore and define our own sacredness, through the exploration of others.

One wonders if the Cro-Magnons had words of consecration, words of creation, and words of proclamation. One also wonders if their prayer was a phenomenon which could easily be observed. It is very probable that their prayer was for security, outward prosperity, and influence over nature just like prayers of today. It may be that the Cro-Magnons were capable of visiting their "spiritual foundation" in order to pursue a divine decision during their sacred moment, much like people of today.

As mankind has risen in civilization, its sacred moments have risen with it; degree by degree toward a higher and purer conception of divine power. In the sacred moment, self ascends to a higher dimension in the cosmos and engages in the highest spiritual activity and realizes its infinite being, supernatural power, and divine strength.

The sacred moment is a victory over finite dependence and finite distress, for it has the power to raise up. to illuminate, and give order to that region called the self, and thus advance the cause of moral dimensions of human existence.

There is a feeling of divine presence and a sense of enactment by the self which is similar to the presence of an artist at his or her work of art. One comprehends the creativeness of the universe and humanity and endeavors to advance the created status of one's self and that of others. One becomes the receptor of infinite reason pouring out its light to finite reason and consciousness.

Max Scheler, author of *The Eternal In Man,* wrote:

"In the idea of the divine there is a direct, necessary, and real connection for the religious consciousness between the ens a se, and the all pervading active force and the value-modality known as holiness, with all of its attendant wealth of value-qualities."

The fact that the divine, the holy, and the sacred is so significant to the self points to the fact that self is transcendentally constituted. Evidence of this was also given in God's word's to Moses, "I am that I am. Tell them that the Same sent me.

William Earle, author of the book, *Mystical Reason,* wrote, "The ego which perceives, remembers, desires, anticipates, and entertains transcendental meanings, if only by way of wondering about them, must have a most remarkable structure. As German philosopher and mathematician, Edmund Husserl put it, "the transcendental ego is the wonder of all wonders. Further, this wonder of all wonders is nothing remote from each self at all; it is that self, as it show's itself to itself."

In a similar way, Buddhism states that Atman is the soul or self of all things, including our own self. When Self realizes self through experiences, suffering is ended, ego is minimized, and what is real in our self is maximized.

Buddhism preaches that the real self is Brahman. Christianity declares the path to God is inward in the depths of our soul.

Buddhism declares that the self is not something we should construct. It is already what it must be and is not to be changed or we fall into idealism.

It is like a treasure that is waiting to be discovered. The ego wants to destroy the self so it must be destroyed or reduced. To be rid of sensations, perceptions, impressions, and consciousness itself is to find reality. Immortality is an illusion. When the freed self sees God face to face; it is freed from the fetters of life and grows into omniscience, senses infinity, and sees everything with the eye of the all-self. Egoism and finitude are removed and the infinite remains. Buddhism and Hinduism reject the ego because it is the enemy of spirituality. However, the individual personality is believed to remain after death.

Yoga teachings declare that the mind is a borrowed intelligence and that real intelligence is pure consciousness or the Great Self.

Atman is the breath of the breath, mind of the mind, and eye of the eye. According to Buddhist thought, the world is what we make it, think it, or what we put into our ego. Every mind constructs its world. To reach reality is to transcend it by arriving at union with Atman.

Mystics in many traditions have stated that there is an experience of unity of all things, found in the depth of the individual soul and in the world of nature. It is said that unity can be achieved through meditation and results in joy and harmony.

The soul of all things is my soul and every nature is a Buddha nature is the theme of the *Tibetan Book of the Dead*. It states that heaven, earth, hell, and all phenomena, gods, demons, and nightmares about death are imaginations of the ego and will be removed when we gain knowledge of the true self that says that "That Art Thou." Furthermore, to be joined with God and to realize your true Self is the same Nirvana, the end of all suffering. Generally, the aim of Buddhism is to reach humility and "melt" into the ego less self in humility and freedom. This may be achieved in meditation where one tries to block out thoughts and let one's presence flow over oneself. In the accompanying gaps between presence and absence one should be able to discern the self.

Creation is a meditation or prayer, so to meditate or pray is to be created. Bliss is derived not from receiving things or favors, but from being what we are. In *The Legend of the Baal Sheem*, to be created is to receive ecstasy. "One who sinks into the Nothing of the unconditioned receives the forming hand of the spirit." Those who achieve pure uniqueness achieve pure perfection because ultimate individuality has no "otherness" which can have power over it and so it is redeemed and united with God. S. Kieregaard wrote:

"The law for the development of the self with respect to knowledge, in so far as it is true that the self becomes the self, is this, that the increasing degree of knowledge corresponds with the degree of self-knowledge, that the more the self knows, the more it knows itself. If this does not occur, then the more knowledge increases, the more it becomes a kind of inhuman knowing, for the production of which man's or woman's self is squandered."

In the book, *Confessions,* Augustine describes the "inner life of the inner part" and presents from his past events of spiritual significance which lead him to a transcendental kingdom. In his book, *Naturalism Supernaturalism,* M.H Abrahams describes Augustine's experience as follows:

"Augustine achieved an astonishing subtly in discriminating the variety and nuances of men and women's "affections and the movement of their hearts"; of the complex interaction between what the altering mind brings to perception; of the difficulty of separating the pure fact in memory from the intrusive presence of the self that remembers; and of the slow and obscure growth of convictions and values, which burst suddenly into awareness in the quantum leap of a moment of insight. St. Augustine established the spiritual vocabulary for all later self-analysis and treatments of self-foundation and the discovery of one's identity." His ideas have attracted strong interest among famous philosophers such as Ludwig Wittgenstein, Proust, Joyce, Rousseau, Wordsworth, Marthenius Versfeld, Traherne, and others.

Augustine mentioned that mankind could enter a time when it was stripped of significance by false concepts and human activities could be stripped of all meaning. The quality of our being rests on the quality of our desires. Our being is in a state of becoming as we discover and become aware of new concepts and truths.

The Greeks became aware that love of friendship overthrows tyrannies. Marthenius Versfeld wrote that Plato in his Symposium "Set out a scale of loves, each lower love being taken up into a higher love until the form of Beauty was seen with inward eye, as something in all loves. Augustine, even more than Plato knew that men and woman desire an ultimate fusion of love and intelligence." Augustine's *Confessions* took the collective evil of mankind and transferred its concern to the wrongdoing of the individual self and it became a path to personal redemption through suffering. The experiences of pain, doubt, terror, and depression can lead to successive growth of mind and even interaction with nature that results in cumulative self-knowledge, self-formation, self-recognition, self-coherence and self-love.

The philosophers, poets, artist, and writers are like physicians who heal the painful experiences of the mind as mentioned above by providing balm and a fusion of intelligence for bruised consciousness. Poets, writers, artists, and philosophers deliver men and women form alienation from nature, alienation from others, and alienation from our selves. They remind us that the acquisition oriented ego with its monetary bonds to others in society can be harmful to the plenitude of one's being because it causes alienation and estrangement from others and nature.

The poet, Shelley, wrote In *A Defense of Poetry*:

"The great secret of morals is love, or a going out of our own nature and an identification of ourselves with the beautiful which exists in thought, action, or person, not our own. A person, to be greatly good, must imagine intensely and comprehensively; he or she must put themselves in place of another and of others; the pains and pleasure of his or her species must become one's own. The great instrument of moral good is the imagination…Poetry enlarges the circumference of the imagination."

Keats related a similar idea in his *Endymion*. He sets up a ladder of love which allows us to overcome the limits of self by joining in a communion with essence, friendship, and finally selfless love to a loved one, relatives, humanity, and nature. Shelley described love as "a communion not merely of –the senses but of our whole nature, intellectual, imaginative, and sensitive." This is one of mankind's great needs because men and women are social beings. Yet, they are imprisoned in a wall of personality, a lifeless other where they are cut off from each other and the social order because cash payment has become the chief interaction of man with man woman with woman, and woman with man.

Without love of self or love of others, life can be a plane of despair, a hill of hate, a dead hostile desert. Carlyle describes what life is like without love and communion with others as follows; "Invisible yet impenetrable walls as of enchantment, divided me from all living… It was a strange isolation then lived in. In the midst of their crowded streets and assemblages, I walked solitary… To me the Universe was all void of Life, of Purpose, of Volition, even Hostility."

When man and woman enter the idea of the sacred self and affiliate love, the wasteland and the lifeless world springs to life and gives us the sanction to banish the sick hurry, the divided aims, the strange disease, the brokenworld that has ensnarled us, and restore the feeling of wholeness, the feeling of community, and the wealth of previous development- all of which are our birthright. The reunion of man with man, woman with woman, and man with woman with nature, offers a resurrection of man and woman and a resurrection of nature D. H. Lawrence stated it well in his book *Apocalypse:* "We and the cosmos are one. The cosmos is a vast living body, of which we are still parts.

What men and women most passionately want, is their living wholeness and their living unison. We ought to dance with rapture that we should be alive and in the flesh, and part of the living organic connections, with the cosmos, the sun and earth, with mankind and nation and family. Start with the sun, and the rest will, slowly, slowly happen."

The omnipotence of our mind over matter can be a lightning bolt that reveals a new edifice. Let every faculty of mind be awakened. Let every feeling be raised in intense interest. Let every principle and passion, receive infinite inspiration.

We must be on guard lest these expectations be blown away in an existential hurricane as they have been before. Let man and woman, create a world with a spiritual biography, a Golden Age without and a paradise within. The mind of men and women has confronted the old social framework with the power of revolution. Now it is time to exercise the power of self-consciousness and unleash a new spirit of millenium excitement in which external means give way to internal means.

In his *Fragment von Hyperion*, Holderlin described the mind of man and woman as having two opposing motivations; the motivation due to acquisition and the motivation due to power. When these motivations turn to the negative side, man or woman, want to either control everything, or enslave everything.

M.H. Abrams wrote: "The stage of man's or woman's "highest self-development." will consist in achieving an "organization of these opponent motivators" in infinitely multiplied and strengthened forms". The poets have long cried out for transformation. Wordsworth wrote an ideal version of such a transformation:

"There was a mighty change… and from that moment the contest assumed the dignity, which it is not in the power of anything but hope to bestow… from that moment "this corruptible put on incorruption, and this mortal put on immortality."

This hope is manifested in the stirring of the self, the Expansion and Contraction of the organs of Perception, the Translucence of Consciousness and a Chain of Linked Thought such as the following:

> The sacred self is stirring to give
> The world another heart and another start.
> Pulses of life beat like a projected art.
> In the woods and cities uplifted voices live;
> Creating Time, Creating Space
> With Visionary forms for the human race.
> Lo, from the Human Imagination
> A great and glorious birth,
> Calls forth a new determination to arise on earth.
> It is the modern sacred moment,
> Filled with revelations and inspiration,
> Distinctive regeneration and exultation,
> Metaphorical translation and intellection.
> ---R.J. Choura

Friedrich Schlegel stated that: "Real living is an eternal becoming, engendering endless fullness and diversity."

Self sets itself in motion and develops a wealth of moments. It is said that when a person knows the self, knowledge becomes more of a treasure than charms of this world. For a person who has realized the self, the temporal world of phenomena and emotions is "Like the illusion of silver in mother of pearl, the world appears to be real only until the Supreme Self, the immutable reality behind everything is realized."

In the *Atma Bodha Sankara,* the Great states that, "Knowledge of Self is the only direct means to liberation. As cooking is impossible without fire, so is liberation without knowledge of the self. Knowledge of self surely destroys ignorance, as light destroys the densest darkness."

We may ask what is the aim of our knowledge of self? One answer is to have life and have it more abundantly. We may ask why? The answer is that the sole source of values which we know in the universe is the relationship between the self and matter and what we call life. Man and woman are infused with matter and energy, the "universal world stuff," and are capable of feeling, loving, planning, and seeking the truth.

Marthinus Versfeld wrote: "Morality means the discovery and construction of the world in company with one's fellow men and women, and not in a set of prohibitions and abstractions relative to our ego." The "me" and the abstractions with which it buttresses itself are only opinions. Every man and woman are naturally in the truth. A Zenist would say that he or she is a Buddhist; a Christian, Jew, Moslem, or Hindu that he or she is the image of God. In spontaneity, we act out the truth, which is concealed by division and opinion.

In many religions, the most influential root metaphor for describing the relationship of God and the self is the statement that "God is love". In the book, *The Confessions,* by Augustine, there is a ladder of love, which leads to enlightenment. Augustine believed that evil comes from misplaced or perverted love, but at the center of every evil desire there is a spark of love which can be freed to become an honor to God, and a receiver of God's love. We are then capable of seeing and loving the image of God in our neighbor. This then allows us to love our self so that our self- love is God love.

In the play, *The Man for All Season,* Robert Bolt makes the motivating force, which takes Thomas Moore to martyrdom his hero's "adamantine sense of self." He describes Thomas Moore as a man who knew how far he would yield to love and fear, but who was steadfast and unchangeable when at last he was threatened and asked to swear a false oath. Rather than pull back from that final place, where he had "located himself", Thomas Moore died. In the play he says, "When a man takes an oath he's holding his own self in his hands; like water; and if he opens his fingers, then he needn't hope to find himself again."

THE SELF, THE SOUL, AND THE INNER ESSENCE OF THE ETERNAL

By seeking the Truth of our Being and the beautiful, in infinite variations(through spiritual, poetic, artistic, and musical beauty) helps us to see the Eternal in things. Then, even in the dark of night, all Being awakens with the Light by abiding in divine contemplation and keeping the senses in harmony. From the *Arjuna of The Bhagavad Gita* we read: "They say that the power of the senses is great. But, greater than the senses is the mind. Greater than the mind is Buddhi, reason; And greater than reason is He, The spirit in man and woman and in all."

Similarly, from the Indian Sanskrit literature, there is a prayer from the writings in the *Vedas* known as the famous GAYATRI which has been recited every morning for over 3000 years by millions of the faithful of India. They say:

"Let our meditation be on the glorious light of Savitri. May this light illumine our minds."

The mind of India has always searched for the Light. India has given us a complementary view of the world compared to the Greeks. In an Indian temple there is a inspiring sense of veneration and power of Infinity: in a Greek temple there is a sense of the unobstructed perfection of beauty. India presents the spirit with the joy of the Infinite in the inner world;

and Greece presents the spirit with the joy of everlasting beauty in the outer world.

Poet, William Wordsworth, expressed this spirit of India in his poem "*Tintern Abbey*". Poet, John Keats, expressed this spirit of Greece in his poem, "*On A Grecian Urn*".

Many Indian poets and scholars have also expressed the spirit of India in the Sanskrit literature which dates back over 3000 years. Some of it was composed long before writing was introduced into India. It is not associated with tragedy or history like Greek literature. It is composed of romanticism, idealism, useful wisdom, and a passionate desire for spiritual vision. In it mankind is seen watching the glory of the dawn and the glory of the sun with joy and wonder.

Sanskrit literature presents to us knowledge of "that which cannot be seen, cannot be heard, cannot be perceived, cannot be conceived" -in the ordinary sense of these words except by slow by slow degrees from it. Its most remarkable mystical and philosophical texts are as follows:

Vedas- The most important and oldest scriptures of India. These songs are holy writings which are said to be divine revelations received by saints and seers who lived hundreds of years B. C.

They are not dogmas or theology but meditations about overwhelming spiritual experiences and insights into eternal truths.

There are four *Vedas: Rik, Sama, Yajur, and Athera*. Each *Veda* is divided into two parts- Work and Knowledge. They were composed in Sanskrit between 1500 and 500 B. C. and contain the spiritual source of Hinduism. The *Vedas* were written at the dawn of spiritual vision and the dawn of human thought. They ask what was there before heaven and sky- They say that love was the first seed of the soul; that sages found the first bond of unity between being and non-being; that darkness was hidden in darkness.

Our daily life springs from the infinitely renewable source of entropy and makes our very Being part of timeless essence. *The Upanisads-(Breath of the Eternal)*- are The Sacred Books of the East. They were written over several centuries before 500 B. C. and strive-by parable, proverb, simile, and metaphor- to arrive at truth without erecting a formal system. They offer a valuable experience of great thought with deep mystical and existential implications. They created the later wisdom of India and greatly influenced western philosophy from the time of Schlegel, Hegel, Schopenhauer, and Schelling. *Upanisads* is the plural of *Upanisad*.

The *Upanisads* are the bible of the Hindu religion. Literally, it means sitting near devotedly. It also means secret teaching-and is secret because it can only be absorbed by those who are spiritually ready to receive it. It is also interpreted to mean knowledge of God. How many *Upanisads* once made up the greater *Upanisads* is unknown, however, one hundred and eight have been preserved.

The *Upanisads* are concerned with the inner nature of mankind. At the core of the *Upanisads* are the words TAT TVAM ASI: "That thou art:. This refers to the manifestation of what is called Brahman in the soul. Brahman is the ultimate reality and the unifying concept is called Atman. All things and events which surround us are but different forms of the same ultimate reality. Brahman is the Truth of the Universe and Atman is our Inner Truth. There are two names for truth and here they are the same. Atman, and Self is never born, never sick, and never dies.

The spiritual experience of Atman is similar to what is called Cosmic Consciousness or illumination, which will be discussed shortly. *The Chandogya Upanisad* describe it as follows:

"There is a Spirit which is mind and life, light and truth and vast spaces. He contains all works and desires and perfumes and all tastes. He enfolds the universe, and in silence is loving to all."

It goes on to describe Brahman as follows: "This is the spirit that is in my heart, smaller than a grain of rice, or a gain of barley, or a grain of mustard seed, or a grain of canary seed, or the kernel of a grain of canary seed. This is the Spirit that is in my heart, greater than the earth, greater than the sky, greater than heaven itself, greater than all these worlds. This is the Spirit that is my heart. This is Brahman.

He cannot be defined because He is Infinite. "He is seen in the wonder of a flash of lightning. He comes to the soul in the wonder of a flash of vision."

Brahman is a state of consciousness beyond time, thought, and imagination. It is when Being, Consciousness, and Joy are ONE.

In the *Mandukya Upanisad* is an explanation of Brahaman and Atman:

"Brahman is all and Atman is Brahman. Atman, the Self, has four conditions.

The first condition is the waking life of outward moving consciousness, enjoying the seven outer gross elements.

The second condition is the dreaming life of inner moving consciousness, enjoying the seven subtle inner elements in its own light and solitude.

The third condition is the sleeping life of silent consciousness when a person has no desires and beholds no dreams.

The fourth condition is Atman in His pure state the awakened life of supreme consciousness.

It is neither outer consciousness nor inner consciousness, neither semi-consciousness nor sleeping consciousness, neither mere consciousness nor unconsciousness. He is Atman, the Spirit himself, that cannot be seen or touched, that is above all distinctions, beyond all thought and ineffable. In the union with Him is the supreme proof of His reality. He is peace and love. The *Kena Upanisad* says that, "He is known in the ecstasy of an awakening." An awakening is like when you realize a forunate rhythm has been struck by an artist as you view a work of art, and you experience a radiance. That is an epiphany and it is similar to a spiritual experience or awakening in which an all-informing spiritual principle comes through.

Ramakrishna, the India saint of 1836-86,helps us understand the relationship between I am, the Self, Atman, and Brahman with these words:

"There are three different path to reach the Highest: the path of I, the path of Thou, and the path of Thou and I:

According to the first path to reach the Highest, all that is,was, or ever shall be is I, my higher Self. In other words, I am, I was, and I shall be for ever in Eternity."

In the Advaita tradition in Hinduism, the temporal world illusory and ultimate reality is timeless. Underneath the constant change of life's illusions is the unchanging center, which alone is truly real even though the outer world seems to exhibit other realities. In the Hindu religion, each of the great gods may server as a lens through which the whole of reality is clearly seen. There is one reality and one God but the names and forms by which it is known are different. Name and form-nama rupa- are the words used to describe the visible, changing world of samsara and the multiple world of the gods. The *Veda X121, Chandogya Upanisad 3.19,* and *Aitareya Upanisad 1.1* tell us; if all names and forms evolved from an original kernel or seed of the universe, then all have the potential for revealing the nature of the whole.

"According to the second path to reach the Highest, Thou art, O lord, and all is Thine.

In the early Hindu religious traditions, Ramanuja, in the 11th century, stated that the Lord is characterized both by his utter Supremacy and accessibility. In this path, one emphasizes meditation on a form or image of the Lord to affix the mind. The image may take one of five forms. The five forms of the Lord are Supreme form, the powers of the Supreme, the indwelling of the Supreme in one's mind and heart, the incarnation of the Supreme, and an image of the Supreme Lord which is properly sacred.

According to the third path to the Highest, Thou art the Lord, and I am Thy servant, or Thy son or daughter. In this path one strives to know the Lord and the inner essence of all things. Such a knowing may be called Cosmic Consciousness.

Cosmic Consciousness is knowing the essential inner essence of all things, To comprehend this is to experience the cosmic vision known as Brahmic Splendor. It is a sense of the self seeing with intense inner vision the particles and entities which make up the universe in either their material or spiritual essence-blending in harmony, changing from order to order in synchronous love.

This vision was described by Gautama as seeing the "Chain of Causation"; by Dante as seeing the "eternal wheels", and by Walt Whitman as seeing the "measured and perfect motion" of the "procession of the universe". During this vision, there is an awareness of becoming refined and sensitized; and of becoming susceptible to nature's higher and finer influences, of being filled by the consciousness of all creation, of rising and expanding into the Infinite.

There is an awareness of a creative force forever and forever repeating and repeating the same simple and grand rhythmic process to infinity. It is like a process where a grand hymn is filling the universe while Infinite Wisdom and Love is encircling each life- offering pity, tenderness, and sympathy. Another name for this vision is Cosmic Consciousness. A person who has acquired this vision does not desire eternal life- they have it. They have freed themselves on all sides from all yearnings. Salvation lies in occurrence.

By salvation we mean finding harmony with the "universe", the inner part of our nature, our rarely realized heights, our relation with nature and the social world. To a certain extent, self- sacrificing and devoted individuals have achieved salvation for us by eliminating the miseries of epidemics, external catastrophes, famine, psychological guilt, and disease. Life has become less brutish, nasty, and short. However, there is still a need for more illumination, more optimism, more inspiration, and more development of individual lives.

Knowledge is made up of three levels-opinion, science, and illumination. Also, the world of awareness can be separated into Simplified Consciousness, Self Consciousness, and Cosmic Consciousness.

It is said that thought is a preliminary step to Cosmic Consciousness. One must think of the multitude and harmony of things, then the depths of the inner self, then the highest level of ideas, then enter complete forgetfulness of all things in complete silence. For some this has lead to the source of becoming and being, the root of the soul, the divinity of all good, and the Light of Eternity. Achievement of higher knowledge is the ultimate purpose of all beings, and this is the immediate purpose of man and woman.

In Self Consciousness there is a sense of good and evil, a sense of sin and death, there is a desire to reach the heights of beauty and being, for full command of action over one's conditions; there is a desire for unlimited time. There is a desire to escape the restraints of the flux and rise above time, space, and causation. The poet, Shelly, remembering Plato, states in *Adonais:*

"The one remains, the many change and pass:
Heaven's light forever shines; Earth's shadows fly:
Life, like a dome of many-colored glass,
Stains the white radiance of Eternity,|
Until Death tramples it to fragments."

In Cosmic Consciousness there is no sense of sin or death or evil. Soul and body are no longer strained apart but are linked and glorified; and rise up vitalized and energized in every nerve and fiber. Those who have achieved Cosmic Consciousness exhibit ideal aspirations of the most intense kind; their imaginative life predominates completely over their corporeal and mundane life. The world of imagination is infinite and eternal.

William Blake, the poet, wrote: "It is the divine bosom into which we shall go after the death of the vegetated body. This world of imagination is infinite and eternal, whereas the world of generation, of vegetation, is finite and temporal. We are in a world of generation and death, and this world we must cast off if we would be artist such as Raphael, Michael Angelo, and the Venetian painters. If we do not cast off this world, we shall be lost from the world of art."

Blake, who was blessed with Cosmic Consciousness, was casting off this world when he wrote in his poem Auguries of Innocence:

"To see the world in a grain of sand,
And a Heaven in a wild flower;
Hold infinity in the palm of your hand,
And eternity in an hour."

When we enter the world of imagination we get a glimmer of the *Cosmic Consciousness* and say with William Wordsworth in his poem, *The Prelude*:

"Wisdom and Spirit of the universe!
Thou Soul that art the eternity of thought,
That givest to forms and images a breath
And everlasting motion, not in vain

By day or star-light, thus from my first dawn
Of childhood didst thou intertwine for me
The passions that build up our human soul;
Not with the mean and vulgar works of man,
But with high objects, with enduring things
With life and nature purifying thus
The elements of feeling and of thought,
And sanctifying, by such discipline,
Both pain and fear, until we recognize
A grandeur in the beatings of the heart."

William Wordsworth may have been describing Cosmic Consciousness also when he composed these words in 'Lines' a few miles from *Tintern Abbey* an:

"Aspect more sublime; that blessed mood,
In which the affections gently lead us on
Until, the breath of this corporeal body frame
And even the motion of our human blood
Almost suspended, we are laid asleep
In body, and become a living soul:
While with an eye made quiet by the power
Of harmony, and the deep power of joy."

It is from the medium of imagination that a process of development called "individuation" by Carl Jung helps the unconscious change the one-sided ego into the broadly based Self. To imagine is to bring forth affinities that fit our new existence to existing things. Imagination is the "dawn of our being" and, it creates the bond of union between life and joy.

There dwells deep within us the consciousness of completeness with nature. It lies deep in the soul, below all pain, below all the things of life, in a vast quietness, in an infinite sea of calm-which exists without disturbance. In the intense solitude we see into the unfathomable depths in which we float and realize vast and solemn meanings.

SELF, SOUL, AND THE EFFECTS OF ENTROPY

E ntropy is the originating cosmic and primordial energy fluctuation from equilibrium, which occurred at the beginning of the universe at the Big Bang. It is cosmic because it fills the universe. It is primordial because it came into being with space and time. It is the source of changes and the arrow of time which is forward. It is formless and empty and has no bias toward whatever rises or falls. It is the vast and fathomless, formless energy and limitless potential that nourishes the universe and upon which all life depends.

Scientist now believe, that if our world were in equilibrium, we would not be alive to talk about it. It is now thought that a precondition for the existence of biological matter and the present structure of the universe is due to a fluctuation from equilibrium. It is possible to maintain equilibrium condition in a laboratory because one can change the boundary conditions, but among the stars one is dealing with gravity. The pressure gradient inside stars produces internal forces that prevent collapse due to gravity but the equilibrium that is produced is a quasi-stable one. Cosmologist, P.C. Davis, stated, "The free energy of a gravitating system has no minimum, the final state of matter being not one of uniformity, but a black hole entity of apparently infinite entropy."

Most of the entropy in the universe is in the form of primordial photons, which are quanta of radiation. The heat capacity of this radiation is enormously greater than that of matter, and also about a hundred times greater than all starlight.

The amount of entropy that is generated in a star is large but, it is a very small perturbation in the amount of the universe's existing entropy. Yet, it is the non-equilibrium caused by this small perturbation that all life and structure depend. Entropy could be considered as something, which is the cause of an eternal rhythm.

Entropy creates an eternal order. Entropy is associated with the forward direction of time. It gives meaning to the self internally in terms of consciousness and externally in terms of an absolute order of time. This allows order so that actions have a priority and value connected to time.

Physicist, Arthur Eddington maintained that entropy is "an appreciation of arrangement and organization" and therefore deserves to be placed "alongside beauty and melody." He said that entropy may admit only the metrical aspects of things as beauty and melody; but by this limitation it raises "organization" from a vague descriptive epithet to one of measurable quantities of exact science. One may say that what entropy theory measures is not the nature of organization but only its overall product, namely the degree of dissipation of energy it entails, the amount of "tension" available for the work in the system.

Every so often one finds a reference to entropy in relation to the arts and music. Richard Kostelanetz, in an article on *"Inferential Arts,"* quoted Robert Smithson's *Entropy and the New Monuments* as saying of recent towering sculptures of basic shapes that they are "not built for the ages but against the ages" and have provided a visible analogue for entropy."

In 6 B. C., the Greek poet, Solon, wrote a poem, dividing human life into seven-year periods, where each period has its own special function. Each such period in a person's life has special meaning and each period should be in harmony with other such periods. All such periods of life rise and fall with the rhythm of the cosmic code of entropy.

Solon's poem is one of the greatest examples of the Greek sophia or wisdom. The Greek poetry itself contains the essence of rhythm because it is built on a metric system, which allows it to have more rhythmic potentialities than most other languages. Greek metric surpasses English metric because Greek metric is quantitative that is the meter is based on the time it takes to speak it. English metric is determined, by its degree or pattern of stress of musical tone and this is called accentual metric. Accentual metric is not as positive as quantitative metric because its accent or rhythm may vary and be doubtful; whereas in Greek metric, the rhythm is clear and full of intensity from the beginning. Greeks preferred a quantitative metric because they understood that rhythm and harmony expressed in sounds or words; were essential to molding the self or human spirit. There is in the spirit of self a sympathy with sounds which touches the soul and as the ear is pitched, so the mind is pleased. The following poem expresses this:

"The soul of words slumber in a shell,
Till waked and kindled by a master's spell;
Then waiting hearts which touch them soar
With a thousand rhythms unfelt before."

In each period of a person's life there are differences in what we seek. These differences are not due to right or wrong, nor true or false, but are due to different temperaments. Youth relates more to the gladness, fullness, and magnificence of things, while the more mature relate to completeness, sufficiency, and tranquility of things.

The aspect of each approaching day is a mystery, which engages the spirit of mind to call forth the Spirit Of Light. Profound reason seeks profound mystery. When the self receives real vision, it enters the "ether of veneration and communes with the unutterable." Self enters into the All and the idea of All, with the accompanying idea of eternity, the quantum vibrations in all things, pulsating endlessly the eternal beats of life.

Hegel, the philosopher, wrote in his last chapter of the book *Phenomenology*: "Time appears therefore as the destiny and necessity of the spirit, which is not complete within itself; the necessity, to enrich the share which self-consciousness has in consciousness; or conversely, taking this inherent nature, as that which is inward, to realize and make manifest that which is at first only inward-i.e., to claim it in the spirit's certainty of self."

A person's spirit undergoes the process of coming into being in time by the process of knowledge carried forward in time. Such knowledge is often in the form of history. One might say that the goals of history are to help the individual gain knowledge of their self, change their spirit from abstract to concrete, and promote "progress in the consciousness of freedom."

One might say that historians help us to feel time or entropy because they explain the cause and effect of events so that time has precedence over space. They also lead us to an idea of our destiny due to historical orderings of important events. They also relate history to rhythm. Arnold Toynbee wrote: "If human history repeats itself, it does so in accordance with the general rhythm of the universe, but the significance of this pattern of repetition lies in the scope that it gives for the work of creation to go forward.." Also, "The guideline of History is a progressive increase in the provision of spiritual opportunities for human souls.."

Toynbee and other historians felt that there is an alternating rhythm of static and dynamic movement and pause, which is part of the fundamental nature of the Universe. Historians show us the progressive fulfillment of the nature and purposes of the spirit. Historians are exact, unbiased, sincere, impartial, free from fear, resentment or affection, and faithful to the Truth. History strengthens the soul of a nation and solidifies its people. Historians show us how the good we enjoy or the evil we suffer is related to the past so that we may impart precision, definiteness, and solidity to our spirit. Some have said that this is the, most pleasant school of wisdom because it makes amends for the shortness of our lives.

Caryle wrote, "History is the first distinct product of man and woman's spiritual nature, their earliest expression of what could be called thought." History gives us the epiphanies of entropy so that time and space are not doomed to fade into shadows. History bestows upon us the progress of the human mind, the scaffolding of reason, and the useful intellectual changes in the elegant arts and sciences. From history our souls may win a new world crown. Entropy imparts "not only negative factors but also the positive becoming, all-creating Chronos."

Everything we know in the universe from suns to galaxies, and man and woman to atoms, either rises or descends, evolves or degenerates, develops or decays. Nothing evolves mechanically except degeneration and destruction. That which has consciousness evolves, that which does not, degenerates. It is surprising and fascinating that life on earth has been evolving on an ever, upward scale in spite of the law of entropy which states that everything dissociates into a lower scale and to disorder.

It may be said that entropy is a matter of decreasing energy and that this energy flows to us and through us from the ray of creation. This energy flows to each of us individually and is received as a series or collection of different perceptions, which succeed each other with an incredible rapidity, and are in a constant change and movement. These perceptions fill our minds with ideas. The matter of knowledge flows from our senses and the form of knowledge is furnished by our understanding. These perceptions are bounded by space and time, are related by cause and effect, and are interconnected by forms of intuition, the categories of understanding, and the ideas of reason. In many perceptions, we know the appearances of things but not the things themselves.

Kant wrote in *The Critique of Pure Reason*, "The understanding prescribes laws to nature, and even makes nature possible." The understanding imparts to objects the data from the senses and connects them according to laws. There are certain fundamental laws which are the same everywhere in the world and which work the same in the world and in man and woman, and which point to a fundamental unity in all things and in phenomena of different orders. P.D. Ouspensky tells us in his book, *In Search of the Miraculous*, "The number of fundamental laws, which govern all processes both in the world and in man and woman is very small. Different numerical combinations of a few elementary forces create all the seeming variety of phenomena.

The first fundamental law of the universe is the law of the three forces of the three principles, and is called the "law of three." It states that every phenomenon in the universe results from the simultaneous application of the positive, negative, and neutralizing forces.

The next fundamental law of the universe is the "law of seven or the law of octaves." It states that the universe is filled with vibrations that spring forth from infinite directions, crossing each other, bumping each other, reinforcing or weakening each other. The force that starts each vibration does not act uniformly but accelerates and decelerates, strengthening and weakening in a periodic manner, leaving its original channel and then returning to it again and again. The periods of action are not uniform and the vibrations are not symmetrical. One period is shorter, another is longer."

The law of seven or law of octaves is manifested in the laws of light, heat, chemicals, magnetism, music, and other categories. It is manifested in the period in which vibrations are doubled in frequency from say 1000 to 2000 cycles per second can be divided into eight unequal steps called an octave or made up of eight. It is believed to be a formula of a cosmic law, which supposedly was encoded in music by ancient scholars. It points out in a new way that due to the moment of retardation of vibrations, progress and development of all phenomena in the universe and in nature are subject to intervals which prevent phenomena from traveling in straight lines. At the moment of retardation or change, a change from the original direction takes place, sometimes it may be 180 degrees.

Sometime the change is too gradual to grasp. Other times, it is a broken line! And, this is the way it is with ourselves and society. There is a change of entropy of the self and society in general.

P.D Ouspensky stated:

"After a certain period of energetic activity or strong emotion or a right understanding, a reaction comes, work becomes tedious and tiring; moments of fatigue and indifference enter into feeling; instead of right thinking a search for compromises begins; suppression, evasion of difficult problems. But the line continues to develop though not in the same direction as at the beginning. Work becomes mechanical, feeling becomes weaker and weaker, descends to the level of the common events of the day; thought becomes dogmatic, literal. Everything proceeds in this way for a certain time, then again there is reaction, again a stop, again a deviation. The development of the force may continue but the work, which was begun with great zeal and enthusiasm, has become an obligatory and useless formality. A number of entirely foreign elements have entered into feeling-considering vexation, irritation, hostility; thought goes round and round in a circle, repeating what was known before, and the way out which had been found becomes more and more lost."

This change in interest, attitude, emotion, feeling and thought is a manifestation of the cosmic law, the law of seven, or the law of octaves. It shows how entropy changes from strong to weaker or vice versa. It is part of all domains of human activity.

In many important human activities such as art, fashion, music, literature, design, philosophy, religion, in each person's life, and especially in society in general; there is a development of forces changes from the original direction into the opposite direction, and all the time under the same guise or category. A look at history will reveal this over and over again in the form of love tuning to hate, of conservatism turning to liberalism, of depression turning to inflation, and vice versa.

The above mentioned law of seven in our life has been sounding across the centuries; altering opinions, changing attitudes, changing creeds, turning vices into virtues, and paradoxes into axioms. Coleridge might say that the law of seven teaches us! "But passion and party blind our eyes and the light which experience gives is a lantern on the stern which shines only on the waves behind us." But, being aware of the law of seven we can put the lantern on the bow to shine in front of us and guide us.

The law of seven causes some events to be represented on a large scale and some to be diminished. The law of seven gives us the extraordinary events, the drama of moving revolutions, the surprises of moral epics, the successive advances in technology, the advancement of the human mind, and the revolutions in men and women's spiritual nature. History is man's earliest spiritual expression of the awareness of the results of the law of seven but not the law itself. Through the ages, in nations or groups, the evolution of society is seen to exhibit a recurrent pattern of growth and decline. Ideas are seen to rise and grow and then an exhaustion of ideas sets in. Over time, an alteration of divergent and convergent ideas takes place in society and nations. Facts are collected so that they become information. Information is fitted into context until it becomes knowledge. Knowledge is applied to experience until it becomes wisdom.

As this knowledge is applied, the law of octaves is acting so that there is a deviation of forces first. Secondly, there is a bunching of new discoveries, ideas, applications, and the world is changing. Some things are developing others are weakening and degenerating.

Driving forces are causing recovery or innovation and some paradigms are being worn out. Thirdly, rising and descending octaves are constantly occurring causing manifestations in the life field. Nothing develops without going through an ascent or descent or interval-like waves or a pendulum.

In conjunction with this, inside the self of man and woman there may be dozens and dozens of "pendulums" which cause feelings, reason, and desire to go through mood swings and periods of strength and weakness without any apparent reason. The periods of ascent, descent, and even interval may be periods of development or degeneration in which energy, entropy, and information are increased or decreased. However, P.D. Ouspensky stated that:

"Nothing can develop by staying on one level. Ascent or descent is the inevitable cosmic condition of any action. We neither understand nor see what is going on around us and within us, either because we do not allow for the inevitability of descent when there is no ascent, or because we take descent to be ascent. These are two of the fundamental causes of our self-deception. We do not see the first one because we continually think that things can remain for a long time at the same level. And we do not see the second level because ascents where we see them are in fact impossible as it is to increase consciousness by mechanical means.

Upon the law of octaves in its three principal manifestations depend many phenomena, some of which are psychic, others may be mundane. Upon the law of octaves depends the imperfection and incompleteness of our knowledge in all spheres without exception, mainly because we always begin in one direction and afterwards without noticing it proceed in another."

When we become aware of something about ourselves, our consciousness, or life in general, there is a difference of entropy before and after our knowing. This change in entropy is accompanied by discontinuities and rate changes, which results in organic evolution of the self. Similarly, in cultures and societies, discontinuities and rate changes will result in evolution of culture or society, or a new economic or political condition. This may be accompanied by new opportunities and restructuring.

The force field, which causes the change in entropy, contains properties such as incremental sensitivity to variation in: waveform and pulsation, inner instability of symmetry to yield a new time space framework; plus positive, negative, and neutral forces. Changes in the force field may emanate spontaneously from within or from an external trigger or ripple effect, which generates a new framework. Most changes are due to nonlinear, reciprocal reactions of the constituents of the force field. Such changes are true of living and nonliving frameworks. From these properties evolution occurs in behavior, functions, and frameworks like biological organisms, and brings islands of order amidst seas of chaos. Order occurs at a critical point of challenges and opportunities and causes an amplification of a choice opportunity and a reduction in competing opportunities. This can result in learning by insight instead of trial-and-error, and is a restructuring of the cognitive field.

Information begets the potential for new information and excites processes that are inherent in the learning process. The idea of entropy, which is encompassed in the second law of thermodynamics, has large ramifications in science and philosophy.

It seems like an idea that was originated from the mind of Zeus. It has proven to be worthy of the attention of astronomers, physicists, theologians, chemists, biologists, philosophers, engineers, scientists, and readers and writers of today. It is one of the ways that science has been brought into the life of religion.

The idea of entropy is embedded in the concept of words like God, creation, time, eternity, infinity, and genesis. It is connected with ends and beginnings-and creation's origin and end-matters, which hardly anyone especially theologians and philosophers or scientists would want to sidestep. It is connected with the personal and the planetary and has lead to the idea that time has direction.

Henri Bergson referred to the second law of thermodynamics as the most metaphysical principal in science because it implied that time had a beginning. Freud and Jung deducted that it would imply an energy charged world that was waiting to discharge on man and woman as an energy-bound "pyschic energy" that might create traumatic neuroses, cathartic energy, reduced libidos, or the death wish.

When it was first formalized, the second law was very open to potential interpretations. Lord Kelvin said that it should not apply to living organisms. Svante Arrhenius, the Swedish chemist, thought that it could include the rebuilding of worlds. Emile Meyerson stated it was the death knell of the mechanical explanation of the universe. Williams James suggested that it might be associated with the millennium where everyone is so happy and perfect that they can no longer stand it.

The second law of thermodynamics was discovered in 1824 by Sadi Carnot-a young French engineer. It states that heat flows from hot to cold and that there is more energy that is used by a machine that it can render. Some energy is wasted in friction and some is wasted in wear. In 1850, Rudolph Clausius developed a basic principle from this idea. He said that there is available energy and unavailable energy. The unavailable energy is called entropy.

This became known as the Second Law of Thermodynamics, and it stated that entropy is always increasing. At the beginning, Clausius provided a good start. He concluded that the energy of the world is constant and that the entropy of the world tends toward a maximum. This also meant that the world was moving in a direction from yesterday to today to tomorrow.

R. Emden wrote that entropy was the designer and the director of the gigantic natural processes, and that energy conservation was the bookkeeper.

Ludwig Boltzmann, in Austria, proposed a brilliant new interpretation to what happens to a machine or the universe. Boltzmann said, "When energy is degraded, it is the atoms that assume a more disorderly state; and entropy is a measure of that disorder." This was a profound conception at the time because there were so many anti-atomic doctrines and beliefs at that time.

Boltzmann was the one man who stood up to propose that atoms were as real as our own world. Boltzmann said that disorder could be measured. It is the probability of a particular state or it is the number of ways the particular state can be assembled from its atoms. He gave it the formula:

S=K(log W) where S, the entropy, is proportional to the logarithm of W, the probability of a given state.(K being the proportional constant which is now called Boltzmann's constant.)

It is true that disorderly states are more common than orderly states. But, since Boltzmann's formula is a statistical formula, it actually means there is only a tendency for an orderly system to become disorderly and run down. It doesn't mean it always becomes disorderly. It means that order can also be built up in many places, stars, planets, people, and you and I. In many cases, we see nature working step by step to build up that which is orderly and stable. Atoms form molecules which form bases, which help the formation of amino acids, which form proteins, which help build cells. Cells become simple animals and also more complex animals.

Jacob Bronowski wrote in *The Ascent of Man*:

"Evolution is the climbing up a ladder from simple to complex by steps, each one of which is stable in itself. Since this is very much my subject, I have a name for it: I call it Stratified Stability. That is what has brought life by slow steps but constantly up a ladder of increasing complexity-which is the central progress and problem in evolution. And now we know that that is true not only of life but of matter.

If the stars had to build a heavy element like iron, or a super-heavy element like uranium, by the instant assembly of all the parts, it would be virtually impossible. No. A star builds hydrogen to helium; then at another stage in a different star helium is assembled to carbon, in another star to oxygen or to heavy elements; and so step by step up the whole ladder to make the ninety-two elements in nature."

Friederich Schlegel wrote: "True philosophy finds the highest reality only in an eternal becoming in an eternally living and moving activity which, under ever changing forms and shapes, engenders an endless fullness and diversity."

A similar idea was expressed in the eleventh century by the famous Chinese Confucian philosopher, Zhou Dun-yi, who wrote in *An Explanation of the Diagram of the Great Universe*: "It is The Ultimate of Non-being and also the Great Ultimate (Tai-ji)! The Great Ultimate through movement generates yang. When its activity reaches its limit, it becomes tranquil.

Through tranquility the Great Ultimate generates yin. When tranquility reaches its limit, activity begins again. So, movement and tranquility alternate and become the root of each other, giving rise to the distinction of yin and yang, and the two modes are thus established.

By the transformation of yang and its union with yin, the Five Agents of Water, Fire, Wood, Metal, and Earth arise. When these five material forces (qi) are distributed in harmonious order the four seasons run their course.

The Five Agents constitute one system of yin and yang, and yin and yang constitute one Great Ultimate. The Great Ultimate fundamentally is the Non-Ultimate. The Five Agents arise, each with its specific nature.

When the reality of the Ultimate of Non-being and the essence of yin, yang, and the Five Agents come into mysterious union, integration ensues. Qian (Heaven) continues the male element, and kun (Earth) constitutes the female element. The interaction of these two material forces engenders and transforms the myriad things, the myriad things produce and reproduce, resulting in an unending transformation.

It is man and woman alone who receive (the Five Agents) in their highest excellence, and therefore they are the most intelligent. Their physical form appears and they develop consciousness. The five moral principles of their nature (humanity, righteousness, propriety, wisdom, and faithfulness) are aroused by, and react to the external world and engage in activity; good and evil are distinguished; and human affairs take place."

The Taoist (Daoist) of China believe that cosmic energy and rhythm are part of the cosmic self which resides in each one of us. Taoist, Buddhist, and Zen followers believe that each person has the potential to understand life in an objective and unselfish manner and find peace and harmony with all things. The Confucian philosopher, Mencius, stated in the fourth century, "Those who accord with Heaven will live, those who oppose Heaven will die."

Our world is a living system which requires mutual consideration because of the existence of deeply mutual dependence. For some this sense of wholeness and interconnection has been missing from their beliefs, but occasional disasters have caused some awareness.

Entropy is something deeply infused in the stars,
the elements, and humanity.
It looks at nature not in an hour but in an eternity.
It is something deeply interfused in creation,
And dwells in the light of setting suns.

Entropy is the source of the infinite awe of the cosmos, of the soul of the night, of the eternal flowing of being to Higher Being, of beauty to higher Beauty. In the river of rhythm of life, which we may call entropy, we may find peak experiences, ecstatic moments of joy, and feelings of oneness in which the self feels creativity and serenity throughout. It is in these moments that the self enters the genius loci which is the divine in nature or spirit of place. Here the self operates in its true creative fashion in heightened awareness, overcoming obstacles, moving through orders of increasing difficulty and vibrant attitude of spirit. Here visions confirm and illuminate one another.

The finite self of men and women longs for the Infinite. The rhythm that moves the stars moves the spirit of man and woman and creates a spiritual gravitation, which attracts their spirits to the Soul of the Universe.

We are drawn to see in Nature the common things and natural events which are miracles and riddles and which have their secret sense. Entropy gives to all shapes a "secret and mysterious soul, and a fragrance and a spirit of strange meaning." Entropy invites us to enrich our self and soul by connecting with the scheme of truth and feeling in all forms of nature the infinite and eternal Being.

REFERENCES

Abrams, M. H. *Natural Supernaturalism*. New York: W.W. Norton Co., 1973

Allert, Beate. *Languages of Visuality*. Wayne State University Press. Detroit, 1996 Arnheim, Rudolf. *Art and Visual Perception-A Psychology of the Creative Eye-The New Vision*. Berkley, Los Angeles, London: University of California Press, 1974 Barnet, Sylvan. *A Short Guide to Writing About Art*. Glenview, Illinois, Boston, London: Scout Foresman and Co., 1989

Barzun, Jacques. *The Use and Abuse of Art*. Princeton, New Jersey: Bollingen Series XXXV. 22, Princeton University Press, 1973

Berman, Morris. *The Renchantment of the World*. Toronto, New York, Sydney: Bantam Books, 1984

Breed, Warren. The Self-Guiding Society (Based on The Active Society by Amitai Etzioni). New York: The Free Press, 1971

Bronowski, J. *The Ascent of Man*. Boston, Toronto: Little, Brown, And Co., 1973 Bucke, Richard Maurice, M. D. *Cosmic Consciousness*. New York: E. P. Dutton, 1969

Bynum, Caroline. *"The Complexity of Symbols" from Gender and Religion*, edited by Caroline W. Bynum, et al.: Beacon Press, 1986

Campbell, Joseph. *"The Power of Myth"*. New York, London, Toronto, Sydney: Doubleday, 1988

Cary, Joyce. *Art and Reality*. Garden City, New York: Anchor books Doubleday & Co., 1958

Cobb, Virginia. *Discovering the Inner Eye*. New York: Watson-Guptill Publications, 1988

Coomaraswamy, Ananda K. *Christian and Oriental Philosophy of Art.* New York: Dover Publications, 1956

Copleston, Frederick. *Contemporary Philosophy.* London: Search Press; New York: Barnes and Noble Books, 1972

Cousineau, Phili (Editor) Lawton, Eric (Photographs). *The Soul of the World.* San Francisco: Harper, A Division of Harper Collins Publishers, 1993

De Beauvoir, Simone. *The Second Sex.* Translated by H.M Parshley. New York: Knopf, 1953, p533

Dewey, John. *Theory of the Moral Life.* New York: Holt, Rinehart, & Winston, 1980 Dobzhansky, Theodore. *Mankind Evolving.* New York: Bantam Books, 1970

Eck, Diana. *Seeing the Divine Image in India.* Chambersburg, PA, : ANIMA Books a subdivision of Conocochheague Associates, Inc., 1985

Eliade, Mircea. *Yoga, Immortality and Freedom.* Princeton: Bollinger Series LVI, Princeton Press, 1969

Emerson, Ralph W. *Self-Reliance and Other Essays.* New York: Dover Publications, 1993; Selected Essays of R. W Emerson, New York: Greystone Press, 1951

Erdman, Irving. Arts and The Man- A short introduction to aesthetics. New York: W.W Norton Co., 1939

Evans-Wentz, W.Y.- Compiler and Editor of The Tibetan Book of the Dead (The After-Death Experiences on the Bardo Plane, according to Lama Kazi Dawa-Samdup's English rendering). London, Oxford, New York: Oxford University Press, 1960

Goffman, Erving. *The Presentation of Self in Everyday Life.* New York: Doubleday, 1959

Grof & Grof. *The Stormy Search for the Self.* Los Angeles: Perigree, 1992

Harding, Esther M. *The "I" and "Not I' ~ A Study in the Development of Consciousness.* Princeton, N. J. : Bolligen Series LXYJX, Princeton University Press, 1965

Hardy, Jean. *A Psychology with a Soul*. London, England: ARKANA, The Penguin Group,1989

Harper, Ralph. *The Existential Experience*. Baltimore and London: The John Hopkins University Press, 1972

Hirst, Paul. *Social Relations and Human Attributes*. London and New York: Tavistock Publications, 1982

Jaspers, Karl. *Man In the Modern Age*. Garden City: Doubleday Anchor, 1957

Laing, R.D.. *The Divided Self* (New York: Pantheon Books a Division of Random House, 1960

Manchester, Frederick. Translator of *The Upanishads- Breath of the Eternal*. New York and Scarborough, Ontario: Mentor Book-New American Library, 1948

Margenau, Henry. *The Miracle of Existence*. Boston & London: New Science Library, 1987

Mascaro, Juan. Translator of the *Sanskrit book Bhagavad Gita*. London, England: Penguin Books, 1962

Matson, Floyd W. *Being, Becoming and Behavior*. New York: George Braziller, Inc., 1967

Melucci, Alberto. *The Playing Self*. New York/Melbourne: Cambridge University Press, 1996

Mounier. *Manifest au service du personnalesne*. Paris, France, Esprit, 1936

Muller, Max. Translator of *The Upanishads(The Sacred Books of the East)*. New York: Dover Publications, 1962

Mumford, Lewis. *The Transformation of Man*. New York: Collier Books, 1966 Negroponte, Nicholas. Being Digital New York: Vintage Books, 1996

Overmeyer, Daniel. *Religions of China*. San Francisco: Harper San Francisco A Division of Harper Collins Publishers, 1985

Otto, Rudolph. The Idea of the Holy: An Inquiry into the Nonrational Factor in the Idea of the Divine and its Relation to the Rational, translated by John

W. Harvey (nd ed.) Oxford University Press, 1950. Also On Numinous Experience as Mysterious Tremendum et Fascians.

Prabhavananda, Swami with the assistance of Frederick Manchester. *The Spiritual Heritage of India (A comprehensive exposition of Indian Philosophy and Religion)*. Hollywood, CA.: Vedanta Press, 1969

Ouspensky, P.D. *In Search of the Miraculous*. New York and London: A Harvest Book Harcourt Brace Jovanovich, 1977

Rosenburg, Morris. *Conceiving The Self*. New York: Basic Books, Inc. Publishers, 1979

Santayana, George. *The Sense of Beauty*. New York: Dover Publications, Inc., 1955 Scheler, Max. *"Basic Character of the Divine" from On the Eternal in Man*, by Max Scheler, translated by Bernard Noble. SCM Press and Harper Row, 1960

Twiss, Sumner B. and Conser, Walter H. editors of *Experience of the Sacred*. Hanover and London: Brown University Press, 1992

Wooley, Penney. *Social Relations and Human Attributes*. London and New York: Tavistock Publications, 1982

Zohar, Danah and Marshall, Ian. *The Quantum Society*. London, England, Bloomsbury Publishing Ltd., 1993

BIO OF RICHARD J. CHOURA

AUTHOR OF
ENRICHMENT OF THE SELF AND SOUL

Richard J. Choura was born in Hartford, Connecticut. He graduated from Marianapolis Prep School in Thompson,Connecticut.

He served four years in the U.S. Air Force. He attended the University of Michigan, Mitchell College, the University of Wisconsin, the University of New Haven and graduated from the University of Hartford in Connecticut with a mechanical engineering degree. Afterward he attained the status of Professional Engineer. He worked as a consulting engineer for many well known consulting engineering firms and Fortune 500 companies in many states.

He is married and has two sons. He has been married to Patricia Blackett, an artist, for the last twenty years. She graduated from the University of Tennessee in Art Education. She was in many major art shows and galleries in Columbus, Ohio, Philadelphia, PA, and San Francisco, CA. She also graduated from the Barnes Foundation in Philadelphia, PA.

He enjoys gardening and reading about transitory ideas that can uplift the age.

INSPIRING QUOTES BY RICHARD J. CHOURA

"Today, the good life, the good society, and even salvation, depend on the proper preparation and presentation of one's self; based on self help, self awareness, self enrichment."

"In addition to their vocation, man and woman need to live creatively in meanings and spirituality."

"Anything which prevents spiritual affirmation causes emptiness and meaninglessness."

"Personality grows in the amount that the self apprehends or discovers value."

"The self is important because it is the most complete expression of our inner nature, our personality, our persona, our individuality, and our spirituality."

"Self is a driving force which can conquer fate, energize free will, power self direction, and increase spiritual value."

"The self is like a mystical supervisor that establishes values."

"If the soul could have become aware of the eternal, the infinite, and the incomprehensible without soulscapes, soulscapes would have never been created. They enable the soul to have "free flight into the wordless.""

"Soulscapes are the right hand of Nature. Nature has given us being, but soulscapes give us soul so that essence exceeds existence."

"In the creative thought there is the sacredness of origin, the holiness of originality, the dew of freshness, the priority of philosophical genius, and the capacity to extract knowledge with an intensity of feeling that no one else has done before."

"Thinking is the dressing up of ideas, is the shaping of the storm into a symbol of mankind's passion, is the forming of life's diverse gyrations into exciting rhythms, is calling the weak and strong to general consecration, is building a path to rainbows and sunsets. Thinking is looking at details beyond the big picture, is finding courage beyond fear, is picking up the pieces and creating a wholeness where none had existed."

"Great thinking is the lifting up of transitory ideas to educate the spirit of the age. The poem, the play, the story carry us out of ourselves into a synthesizing experience where we sense the interplay of words upon each other and we respond to clues, feelings, and emotions. Out of our new thoughts, feelings, and sensibilities we become new works of art.

- Richard J. Choura

INSPIRING QUOTES

"The new work of art does not consist of making a living or producing an object d'art or in self therapy, but in finding a new soul. The new era is the era of spiritual creativity… and soul making."

-Henry Miller

"Every work of art is threefold: an earthly trinity to match the heavenly!

First, there is the Creative Idea, passionless, timeless, beholding the whole work at once …

Second, there is the Creative Energy begotten of the idea, working in time from the beginning to the End.

Third, there is the Creative Power, the meaning of the work and its response to the living soul.

And, these three are each one equally in itself the whole work."

-Dorothy Leigh Sayers

www.ingramcontent.com/pod-product-compliance
Lightning Source LLC
Chambersburg PA
CBHW051211120626
46547CB00013B/1298